PENGUIN BUSINESS
WHAT'S YOUR STORY?

Adri Bruckner is a creative communications professional with experience in journalism as well as PR. She won an award for crisis communications for her work at Central European University. Now based in Barcelona, Adri develops communications strategy and produces storytelling content for corporate and non-profit clients, and is currently working on her first novel.

Anjana Menon runs Content Pixies, guiding global companies on critical content strategy. She is a consultant to CEOs and policymakers, a speaker at global conferences and a columnist. She worked for Bloomberg News in financial centres across two continents, managed and anchored a national TV channel and is a founder–editor of *Mint*. She divides her time between London and Delhi.

Marybeth Sandell has chased corporate news stories around the world, working for Bloomberg in Stockholm, London, Zurich and New York. She taught communications and journalism at the University of North Carolina at Pembroke and is the co-author of *Introduction to Data Visualization and Storytelling: A Guide for the Data Scientist*. Based in Stockholm, Marybeth heads group employee and leadership communications for Electrolux.

What's Your St🎤ry?

The Essential
Business-Storytelling
Handbook

Adri Bruckner   Anjana Menon

Marybeth Sandell

BUSINESS

An imprint of Penguin Random House

PENGUIN BUSINESS

USA | Canada | UK | Ireland | Australia
New Zealand | India | South Africa | China

Penguin Business is part of the Penguin Random House group of companies
whose addresses can be found at global.penguinrandomhouse.com

Published by Penguin Random House India Pvt. Ltd
4th Floor, Capital Tower 1, MG Road,
Gurugram 122 002, Haryana, India

Penguin
Random House
India

First published in Portfolio by Penguin Random House India 2021
Published in Penguin Business 2022

10 9 8 7 6 5 4 3 2 1

The views and opinions expressed in this book are the authors' own and the
facts are as reported by them which have been verified to the extent possible,
and the publishers are not in any way liable for the same.

ISBN 9780143457978

Typeset in Sabon by Manipal Technologies Limited, Manipal

www.penguin.co.in

CONTENTS

INTRODUCTION

What's Your Story?

Everyone has a story. Here's ours. As business journalists, we spent decades sifting through corporate news and trying to select the best stories to write. We didn't have a lot of time to listen or decide. Bombarded by 'news' from companies, the stories had to catch our eye—or our ear—and then we had to sell it to editors. Then came our own storytelling as journalists. We had to produce engaging, accurate and memorable stories for our audiences on a strict deadline.

Then we left journalism and began working as communicators for companies and organizations. We became teachers and mentors too. We learnt that storytelling skills were just as valuable, if not more, in this field of work, because they were scarcer.

Today, in an age where we are all being bombarded with information and trying to communicate on all channels available to us, storytelling has become an essential skill.

So we'd like to share our knowledge with you—how to spot a good story, how to write it in a compelling way, with images and data for impact, and with your audience in mind. Then we'll share how to get it out into the world in the right format, through the right channel, so that your story gets heard!

Digital Doesn't Make It Easier

The world sends more than 300 billion emails each day. It reads 500 million tweets a day. There are 1.7 billion websites and 600 million blogs. Five hundred hours of video are uploaded to YouTube every minute.[*]

As you can see, competition for attention is tougher than ever. How can you cut through the noise? How can you make *your* story the one that should be remembered?

It's not just about using the newest channel or the newest technology. The shiniest new tool still won't make up for a story badly told.

---

[*] Sources: https://techjury.net/stats-about/how-many-emails-are-sent-per-day/#gref, https://www.brandwatch.com/blog/twitter-stats-and-statistics/, https://www.websitehostingrating.com/internet-statistics-facts/, https://www.brandwatch.com/blog/youtube-stats/

Telling a Great Story

The big secret to turning your message into a great story is to think like a journalist, a storyteller, and then speak to your audience. In this book, you'll learn the fundamentals of story structure for corporate news—headlines, context, quotes, data and visuals. Follow these guidelines and your story will be compelling and memorable.

Every Medium Deserves a Story

Regardless of your department or function, you will be able to apply your new storytelling skills to emails, text messages, presentations and pitches, along with social media posts, blog posts, company reports and press releases. You'll be able to use them in presentations, events, opinion pieces, speeches, video, paid content, podcasts and even augmented and virtual reality. You will become a better storyteller with all the tools in your toolbox.

Elements for Everyone

These elements come from multiple disciplines. Writers learn to tell stories. Reporters learn to grab attention with headlines and by asking questions. Marketers learn to stand out with branding and mission statements. Salespeople know how to use persuasion.

Executives understand how to explain the details of their organizations. Leaders know how to show and share their expertise and insights. But few books talk about how to bring all these together.

What You Will Learn

In the first section of this book, you'll learn the basic elements of compelling storytelling. First, we'll help you define your organization's mission, the message you aim to convey and who you'd like to reach with your story. The big-picture stuff. Then we'll delve into the nitty-gritty. How to write a good headline and structure a story as the best journalists, writers and public speakers do. How to use data and images to make your story more exciting, credible and memorable. How to avoid jargon that might alienate your audience. And lastly, how to focus on people, because the best stories are about us humans, aren't they?

Next, in the second section, you can explore the different channels and ways to tell your story. When and how should you approach 'traditional' media? Which of the many social media channels should you use, and how? When is it worth sponsoring content, paying for an advertorial, research or corporate social responsibility projects? Then we'll run through the ins and outs of podcasting and video, including what resources you might need, and when audio and video should be your channels of choice.

The third section pulls it all together for various projects and purposes. Turn yourself or one of your company's leaders into a well-known expert or even an icon. Craft your organization's story into a report. Put on an event that shows what your company does and can do, in a webinar, a webcast or a live event. Learn to pitch your company's experts at events hosted by others. Prepare your company's communications for a variety of crises—being prepared is half the battle won when something unexpected hits. Explore experiential marketing, when you draw your audience, such as customers, into the story, with user-generated content, augmented reality or virtual reality—content types that will soon become mainstream.

You can read this book cover to cover, although there are other ways to use it. We've divided it into sections so you can focus on what you need to know now—hone your storytelling skills, review the channels available to map out what's best for your story, or plan out a project such as an event, a report or a campaign. You can dive into just one chapter at a time as well—the titles should help guide you to what you need.

Examples and Exercises

We can all learn from the successes and failures of others—and those are good stories in themselves. We've collected the best and worst examples in each chapter—from horrible headlines to powerful narratives, winning social media campaigns to crisis communications failures. We hope you'll enjoy reading about the best and the worst, often from the world's best-known companies and leaders.

In addition to learning from others, the best way to learn new skills is to practise. Each chapter will offer ways to take what's explained and try it out yourself. Whether you're a student or a seasoned executive, you might find it helpful, even enlightening, to spend some time with the questions and exercises at the end of each chapter.

After all, with enough exposure and practice, these elements of storytelling will weave their way into everything you do. Regardless of your story and how you deliver it, we hope this book provides you with the essential building blocks for creating stories that are both compelling and memorable.

So, What's Your Story?

Now that you know who we are and what you might learn from this book, let's consider you, the reader. Who are you and why are you here?

You may be a student of communication or business, seeking broad knowledge. You may be an entrepreneur getting ready to shout from the rooftops about your start-up. You may be writing your own blog. You may be running a non-profit that needs a broader audience. Or an executive looking to make a bigger impact. You may be a seasoned professional in one of the many silos of communication and looking to move to another area. Or you may just be curious about corporate storytelling.

Whatever your story, welcome! We certainly have a story, or two, for you.

PART 1

Storytelling Elements

1

Your Message

—Know Thyself—

Overview

The digital revolution has radically changed the environment we communicate in. For centuries, we've passed down stories from one generation to another, sharing our message with friends, families and colleagues, and feeling connected as humans. We've always been good at this.

Yet, today's world of communication seems to be moving at warp speed, creating a cacophony in which misunderstandings, misinformation and mistrust run rampant. In this digital age, we are all shouting. Often to people who have no time to listen. The sheer information overload overwhelms us. We are constantly trying to talk faster with techniques such as tweets, GIFs and memes.

This chapter will help you find and formulate your message in this post-digital revolution world. It will set the foundation for truly knowing your story so you can then learn to package and share it with the world using old and new techniques.

Speaking of the world, surely you don't need or expect the whole world to listen to your story? That's where the audience comes in. This chapter will also help you identify your audience, because when you're telling your story, it's crucial to know who you're talking to.

What Is a Story?

When we talk about the stories that make humans human, we're not thinking only of Grimm's fairy tales, religious texts or *Harry Potter*, although those too happen to sell well. We're talking about heroes facing challenges, finding solutions and celebrating them. Every good story is about a person, or people, with a dilemma or a threat they are able to overcome, using skills, integrity and determination.

Does that sound familiar? Sure. You also have a story, and so does your organization. It's what you believe and what you want your customers and potential customers to believe—about your company as well as its product or service. It's not about product specifications.

Here's an example. Toyota makes cars. But to sell them, Toyota needs to say more than how big or small, how fuel-efficient or fast, and how safe or versatile its cars are. And that is the message beyond the product. One slogan Toyota has used is 'Let's Go Places'. Why? Because it's selling the experience of driving a (Toyota) car. It wants to tell you not what a Toyota is—an assemblage of metal and plastic with wheels and a motor and seats—but what it can do for you. In this case, it's putting the customer as the hero, driving into the sunset. The company makes cars but sells an experience.

This isn't necessarily just marketing. Companies and organizations, or perhaps only good ones, have a mission and an identity that goes beyond the product or service. Companies with clear, believable, concise and meaningful missions can weave them through their communication and their organization.

This way, their mission guides whatever they say, whether it is announcing a new product, a venture capital investment or a stock exchange debut, communicating with employees about benefits, motivating an internal team, developing corporate strategy or managing a crisis. Once you've got your company's mission and identity determined, you can focus on your message.

Let's get started.

On a Mission

What's your company's mission? In other words, what is the overarching goal of your company, beyond simply selling its product? What drives your company and its employees to strive for success?

A mission, preferably encapsulated in one statement, not only describes the organization and what makes it distinctive but also expresses its intent and/or philosophy. It should speak to employees but also to the audience, or the target market of the product.

The ideal mission statement is clear, believable, concise, and meaningful. Let's look at some examples.

Google's mission is 'to organize the world's information and make it universally accessible and useful'. This mission statement is easily understood by employees and the audience, i.e., clear and believable. It's also ambitious, and perhaps even inspiring. With the use of words like 'universally' and 'useful', it gives broader context to the goals and philosophy of the company. Nailed it!

Virgin Atlantic's mission is 'to embrace the human spirit and let it fly'. Concise and meaningful, yes, but a bit beyond believable.

Tesla, meanwhile, aims 'to accelerate the advent of sustainable transport by bringing compelling mass market electric cars to the market as soon as possible'. The 'mass market' bit isn't very believable, given the current price of a Tesla car, but let's hope it's the company's goal to bring the price of electric cars down to earth.

Mission statements don't always work out this well. The 'Our Story' section of chocolate giant Hershey's website talks about the company's dedication to 'connections between people around the world'. On the whole page, there's not one mention of chocolate, only two passing references to 'snacks'. Hershey's mission is vague and grandiose. Any company from an Internet provider to a dating site can be dedicated to 'connections between people around the world'. Hershey's would be better off saying something related to their products and what they hope to achieve with them.

There are plenty more mission-statement fails out there. Online retailer Zappos.com says, 'Our purpose is simple: To live and deliver WOW.' What does that mean? The push to sound catchy made the line miss the mark when it came to saying something about what it does, what it delivers and to whom. This is likely to puzzle employees as well as potential customers.

Retail store giant Walmart's mission statement says, 'We help people save money so they can live better.' That sounds okay at first glance, but does saving money necessarily help us live better? We have to spend money to save money, so are they conflating the two? Is selling cheap stuff the mission, then?

Mission or Message?

So now you're clear on what a mission is. What's the difference between mission and message? A mission, and your company's identity by extension, needs to be present throughout your corporate communications, whether it's a tweet, staff bios on the website, an advertising copy, a video, a sales brochure, a presentation or a blog post. Every communication needs to be infused with this overarching idea.

Your message is what you have to say to your audience today. This can be something about why your audience should buy your product (or donate to your cause or volunteer for your organization), or it can be a piece of news you want to communicate.

Mission	Message
• Reduce greenhouse emissions	• Use paper, not plastic
• Make the world healthier	• Vaccines eradicate disease
• Save dogs from death and disease	• Adopt a rescue dog today

The mission of the World Wildlife Fund (WWF) is to conserve nature and reduce the most pressing threats to the diversity of life on Earth. One message, for example, was a call to action to donate to help save the koalas threatened or injured in the Australian bushfires in 2020.

Communicate, Don't Regurgitate

Now you're ready to sort out your message and how to communicate it. Just like WWF, you want to link the big picture, preserving wildlife diversity, to a specific activity, such as helping save animals in bushfires, and then link that to something that your audience is interested in, such as cute koalas. WWF did a good job, but that's not too hard when you get to help koalas.

Here's a more mundane example (but still with cute animals). A company issued a press release titled '62% of Millennials Would Put Pet's Health before Their Own'. Here you've got something that appeals to millennials, pet owners and anybody interested in health issues. That's a big audience. Interestingly, the headline doesn't mention the company that issued the release.

That's in the first line, though: 'HealthPocket, a free information source designed to help consumers find medical coverage, today released results of a millennial health insurance survey, which found that 62% of millennials would take their pet to the vet before going to the doctor for themselves.' The rest of the release reveals the results of the survey with regard to whether millennials (in the US) have health insurance coverage and what lengths they've gone to in order to get healthcare. There's also a great infographic summarizing the results.

This press release links some real news to a broad audience and positions the company in line with its mission, as a helpful solution to find and choose healthcare insurance without being too sales-pitchy or explicit about the connection. This is a great example of using data to promote your company's mission and activity. We'll talk more about how to use data effectively in Chapter 5, 'Using Numbers'.

Here's a less effective example. Ice cream maker Serendipity tried a bit too hard with this press release: 'Selena Gomez Announces Her Ownership in Serendipity Brands and Serendipity3 Restaurants along with the Introduction of Cookies & Cream Remix Ice Cream.'

Let's look at the message. They really wanted to use Selena's star power by starting the headline with her name, but the company is the one making the announcement. They've packed a bit much in the headline, with Selena's ownership and a new ice cream flavour to boot. In this case, it would be better to choose which piece of news is more important to the company's mission.

Its website describes it as a restaurant 'sweet since 1954' that 'created a super-premium and just-as-decadent line of pints' to bring its decadent desserts 'home to our fans'.

Reading the press release, it turns out that Serendipity's launch of a new flavour is timed with Selena's release of a new single called 'Ice Cream'. So a better headline would have been 'Selena Gomez, Serendipity Team Up to Launch "Ice Cream" Single and New Black & Pink Flavour'.

The ice cream is pink-vanilla and black fudge, in a nod to Selena's collaboration with Korean pop girl group Blackpink. Luckily, entertainment news outlets Variety and Billboard got the story right, with headlines such as 'Selena Gomez Celebrates Blackpink Collab with Special Serendipity Ice Cream Flavour'. That headline is sweet success for Serendipity, but it would have been guaranteed with a clearer story from the company.

We'll talk more about how to write a good headline in Chapter 2, 'Headline Elements'.

Who's in the Audience?

You may be writing a blog post, a press release or a marketing brochure, but pretend for a moment that you're talking on a stage. Who would you want to be in the audience? Investors? Students? Elderly people? Extreme sports aficionados? Wine connoisseurs?

That's what audience means, in corporate storytelling as well as in the theatre. This attention to audience sounds obvious, but think about how many ads pop up in your Facebook feed that aren't relevant to you or your purchasing habits. A lot, right? Or think of a tech gadget or software you've been thinking about buying. When you google it to find out more, do you see stories so deep in jargon that they are useless to you? It's important to write to the audience you want to reach.

You probably have an idea who your audience is, in terms of age range, location, gender, income level, interests and other categories. You can choose them when you're setting up ads on social media, right? Well, that's a good step to take. More than that, however, it's important to be sure you're talking to them when you 'speak' to them, via any medium (video, blog, press release, brochure or web copy) or media (television, social media, print or online media).

Point of View

Don't assume that your audience will be interested just because it's your audience. They may not be listening. They may not have a lot of time either, even if they want to listen. People want to hear about themselves. 'What's in it for me?' is the question you need to answer.

So be sure to be speaking from their point of view. Don't tell them why you want them to buy your product—tell them what your product can do for *them*. Here's an example: A sports club was planning a promotion in which it would plant a tree for every monthly or yearly pass it sold. Sounds like a good marketing idea, right? Well, they proposed the following text for their promotion on their website:

1000 passes = 1000 trees.

Buy 1 pass, pay for 1 sapling. We want to create a more livable environment. We want our children to be able to enjoy fresh air. We want to hear the birds sing for many years to come. It is for that reason that we have decided to buy a sapling for each pass sold at XYZ Sports Club over the next few months, and we will see to their planting as well! In this way, we can contribute to increasing the territory of the woodlands, providing a habitat for our native birds, ultimately working for cleaner air and more oxygen.

That doesn't sound right, does it? Perhaps your reaction was, 'Who cares?' That's because it's speaking from the sports club's perspective—what *they* want, what *they* are going to do and what *they* will achieve. This is a missed opportunity to make the customer a partner in saving the environment! Not to mention it's too long. Here's an edited version:

Buy a pass, plant a tree! From now through November, for every monthly or annual pass you purchase, we'll plant a sapling. While you work out, get fit and relax at XYZ Sports Club, your tree will be growing, producing oxygen and providing a home for birds, contributing to a better environment for the future. Join us for a healthy life and a healthy world.

This way, the *customer* comes first, not the club. The customer is getting a bonus with their purchase, not just handing their money over for the club to buy a tree with. The customer becomes a partner in improving the environment just by going to the gym. Much more of an appealing proposition, don't you think?

It's Storytelling Time

Now that you've got your message and your audience, what story are you going to tell? In the sports club example, the edited version tells a story about someone getting fit and relaxing while their money also pays for a tree to grow and contribute to reversing climate change. The customer is the hero—not only of their own life, because they are getting fit, but a climate change activist as well.

The same is true of the WWF campaign, where, just by contributing, one can heroically save koalas from bushfires. The research about pet owners also portrays them as heroes who put their pets' health before their own. That, in turn, reminds readers to use the company's website to find themselves some health insurance.

People want to hear about people. That's why you enjoy a Nike advertisement, or ad, with regular people or professional athletes enjoying sports and inspiring you to 'Just Do It'. By the same token, you aren't likely to be motivated to do laundry by an ad that just shows that detergent X gets things cleaner than detergent Y. But if the people using detergent X are doing things you also like to do, in clean and sparkling clothes you'd also wear, the content is speaking to you.

We'll go into how to write or record people stories in Chapter 7, 'Keeping It Human', including how to interview and connect the story to your product, mission or message.

Exercises

1. Decide which of the following statements are missions and which are messages. Try to guess which company they represent:

   a. *Our customers' favourite place and way to eat and drink.* As we celebrate forty years of [signature product name here], we are looking at the ways this beloved icon has provided feel-good moments for families around the globe.

   b. *Keeping the home team healthy and active.* Striving to be the global leader in the sporting goods industry with brands built on a passion for sports.

   c. *Bringing transportation—for everyone, everywhere.* Get in the driver's seat and get paid.

2. Which of the following messages are expressed with the audience in mind, and which solely represent the company's perspective?

   a. US Potato Farmers Share the Best Ways to Store Potatoes

   b. Are You Ready to Doodle Your Stress Away?

    c. Igloo Introduces Modern Automatic Cat Litter Box That Makes Both Cats and Owners Happy

    d. Domino's Pizza Announces Business Update

    e. Godiva Announces the Lady Godiva Initiative, Honouring Its Namesake

3. Can you help Hershey's chocolate make a better 'connection'? Hone their mission statement from 'Built on connections between people around the world'.

4. Pick a company from your country or hometown. Visit its website and communication channels. What is its mission? Message? Where did you find it? How was it clear to you? If it wasn't, how can you improve it?

2

Killer Headlines

—A Headline That Snoozes, Loses—

Overview

Now you know what your overall mission is, what your message is and whom you'd like to reach. In other words, you know what your organization is about, what you have to say and who you want to read your story.

But how do you say it? The next two chapters will focus on crafting the story. This one starts with addressing how to grab attention with the headline. That's where you hook them so you can reel them in to read your story. Then, we will address story elements in the next chapter.

Headline-writing is an art as old as the news business, but it has taken on special significance in the age of email, instant messaging and social media. Attention spans are short, so you've got to grab your reader's eye with the first few words before they scroll right past. This applies to email subject lines, tweets and other communications as well.

This chapter will provide some insight into the tricks of the trade, so to speak, with examples of how to transform a boring headline into an engaging one. It's not all art, there's some science to it too. It's all about word choice and a little grammar. If you want that click, you've got to get the headline right.

The Headline Is Paramount

How important is a good headline? Well, have you ever shared an article on social media without even reading it? Most of us do this on a regular basis. The satirical news website the Science Post tested this in 2016 by posting the following headline: 'Study: 70% of Facebook Users Only Read the Headline of Science Stories before Commenting'. Almost 46,000 people shared the post.[*]

The thing is, below the headline there was no comprehensible text, only lorem ipsum, the

---

[*] Caitlin Dewey, '6 in 10 of you will share this link without reading it, a new, depressing study says', *Washington Post*, 16 June, 2016, https://www.washingtonpost.com/news/the-intersect/wp/2016/06/16/six-in-10-of-you-will-share-this-link-without-reading-it-according-to-a-new-and-depressing-study/

gobbledygook that publishers use as dummy text before the real content is added. A study by Columbia University and the French National Institute for Research in Digital Science and Technology confirmed that this sharing-without-reading behaviour is rampant—59 per cent of links shared on social media have never actually been clicked on.* Twitter has responded with a prompt asking if you've read the story before retweeting.

Nevertheless, the tendency to share without reading shows how important the headline is. Upworthy, which is known as a 'viral' content site, considers twenty-five headlines for every single piece of content. They choose the best one—the one they think is the most likely to be shared. Upworthy claims to have 50 million visitor engagements every month, so perhaps it's worth listening to their advice on working hard to get the headline right.

Characteristics of a Good Headline

Generally, a good headline uses the active voice. That means the subject is doing the action indicated by the verb.

'Mayor Calls for Action on Climate Change' is in the active voice, whereas 'Climate Change Action

---

* The report can be accessed here: https://hal.inria.fr/hal-01281190/document

Advocated by Mayor' is in the passive voice. The first headline is more engaging and exciting.

If there is detail that indicates that the climate change action is more important, then it could work. 'Climate Change Action Named Top Priority by Mayor After Hurricane' for example.

Another thing about verbs. Use one. An exciting one, because you want your story to happen, not just sit there like a noun. Use the present or future tense, so that you're not recounting history but getting your reader in on the action.

It matters what verb you choose, too. It needs to convey movement, novelty and nail the point of the story.

Speaking of getting to the point, never 'announce'. If you're putting out a piece of news, you're already announcing it. Here's an example. Of the two headlines below, which is better?

'Best Foods Announces Plans to Merge with Quality Shop to Form New Grocery Giant' or 'Best Foods to Merge with Quality Shop to Form New Grocery Giant'?

The same goes for events. Simply having an event is probably not news, unless you are a city that's won the right to host the Olympics. 'Joe's Furniture to Host Furniture Convention' is boring. 'Joe's Furniture to Bring 100 Major Manufacturers to Cincinnati' or 'Joe's Furniture, 100 Major Manufacturers to Develop Sustainability Strategy' might get more to the heart of the matter.

Keep It Simple

Use the simplest words possible. For example, use 'use', not 'utilize'; and 'show' instead of 'demonstrate'. You can leave out articles such as 'a' and 'the' as well as auxiliary verbs such as 'is [planning]' or 'have [reached]'. In this case, use present tense, such as 'plan', 'reach' or a clearer verb such as 'agree'.

Readers are drawn to headlines that give context, in time or space or rivalry, especially with superlatives, such as 'first', 'biggest' or 'worst'. Research shows that negative headlines get more clicks than positive ones. That's hard to swing when your restaurant wants to announce that it's been named the best seafood spot in your city, but it can be done on corporate blogs, for example, with headlines such as a travel management company saying 'How to Avoid Wasted Time and Budget in Business Travel'.

Another way to spark interest is to ask a question, such as 'Just How Badly Can Coronavirus Mess Up the Stock Market?'

With questions, it's important to spark interest and remain believable. Avoid questions with simple answers (How Old Is Betty White?) and stay away from fear tactics (Is Your Fatigue a Sign You Have Cancer?). What you can do is set up an answer in the headline, as in 'Why Are Kittens So Cute? Science Will Tell You', or ask a question that your company can answer, such as 'What Makes a Cricket Ball Fly Farther?'

Search and You Will Find

Of course, you'll need to consider search engine optimization (SEO) in your choice of headline as well. SEO is how to use words, design and links on a website or a piece of content to make it rank high on a search engine's list of results—in the unpaid section, also known as organic listings. Ideally, you want your content to be among the top five items in a Google search for the topic you're writing about. Why? Because the top five items get 70 per cent of the clicks on Google searches.[*]

So, you need to write headlines that not only sound good and put your point across, they should also rank high in search-engine results. For this, you'll need to use keywords, which are the words people type into the Google search box.

There's a whole science behind this, and search engines adjust their algorithms often, so you can rely on one of the many agencies specializing in SEO to help you out. Before you seek one out, you can learn the basics.

How do you know what keywords to consider? Do your research. Pretend you're a member of your audience, i.e., a potential customer, the person you want reading your content. Think what they might

---

[*] Matt Southern, 'Over 25% of People Click the First Google Search Result', Search Engine Journal, 14 July 2020, https://www.searchenginejournal.com/google-first-page-clicks/374516/#close

search for and type it into Google's search box, but don't press 'Enter'! See what pops up as similar searches. Also scroll down to the list 'People also search for' and look at those words. In a nutshell, these are the words and phrases you should consider putting in your headline.

If you want help with finding out what people search you can try tools such as Answer the Public, which will tell you what words they use. And you can do a deeper SEO dive by using a site such as SEO Analyzer, Semrush or Moz to automatically analyse content you've already got online. These will help you improve your SEO and give you a better sense of the ideal keywords.

Unfortunately, it's not as easy as stuffing your headline with keywords. If you do that, you may lose the news value or the uniqueness of your headline. Some algorithms penalize you for too many popular keywords.

If your news or blog post is relevant and newsworthy, it should naturally include words that people search for. That's also another reason to use simple words—those are what people type into search engines.

When you do use keywords, make sure they are at the beginning of your headline, if possible. Search engines usually display just 64 characters before cutting to the results.

One last tip on SEO. If you google 'google on SEO', the first result will be a starter guide created by Google. It's a page you want to visit often to stay up to date on what the leader in search is saying about SEO.

Don't Make Readers Feel Fooled

Getting the headline right also means avoiding overkill, or you'll end up with clickbait. Clickbait is a sensationalized headline, often exaggerated, shocking or just plain false, which is designed to entice people to follow a link. The content in the article doesn't back up the claim in the headline.

For example, any headline with 'mind-blowing' or 'you won't believe it' in it, or multiple exclamation points, is suspect. Sites such as BuzzFeed live off such headlines, focusing on maximizing traffic rather than actually delivering 'mind-blowing' content, although they have reined in this tendency of late.

Take this example. 'After You Read These 10 Food Facts, You'll Never Want to Eat Again!' It's all well and good to encourage healthy eating. But it's not likely that people will never want to eat again. That makes this particular headline a flat-out lie.

Speaking of lying, it's important to state your news rather than using clickbait-type techniques that manipulate the reader. '10 Ways to Lose Weight Now: #9 Will Shock You!' is annoying and forces the reader to click if they really want to know what #9 is, but they are not likely to respect you for making them do that.

Clickbait has become so widespread that Google has altered its algorithms to penalize content for it.

So, what's a better headline than '#9 Will Shock You'? Put the real news in the headline: 'New Superfood

May Spark Weight Loss Success' is clear and enticing. (A new superfood? Weight-loss success? Cool!) But it's still mysterious enough to prompt a click.

Not all lists such as the one above are clickbait. So-called listicles (short for 'list articles') are very popular and may garner you lots of clicks, as long as you don't mislead the reader. 'How to' and 'Here's Why' headlines also spark curiosity and promise to answer searchers' questions. You can learn more about how to write good listicles in Chapter 3, 'Story Alchemy'.

Less Is More

Brevity is key. News sites such as the BBC, arguably one of the most authoritative and credible news sources in the world, try to squeeze a whole headline into as few as 34 characters, and just six or seven words.

'Bloomberg Joins Democratic Debate amid Poll Surge' and 'Human Compost Funerals "Better for Environment"' are two BBC examples. With these two headlines, you don't need to read the article to know what's being conveyed, but you will if you're interested in the topic.[*]

More analytical pieces deliberately keep some information back. Feature-story headlines are meant to entice you to click by offering a question or a promise

---

[*] Jakob Nielsen, 'World's Best Headlines: BBC News', Nielsen Norman Group, 26 April 2009, https://www.nngroup.com/articles/worlds-best-headlines-bbc-news/

of more in-depth information: 'Should Kidney Donors Be Paid?' and 'How Mattresses Could Solve Hunger' are two BBC examples. We'll explain more about feature stories in Chapter 3, 'Story Alchemy'.

Once you've written a series of headlines, you can decide which one is best by using the rule of thumb that most journalists follow, known as TACT: Taste, Attractiveness, Clarity and Truth. Ask yourself if your headline is tasteful (meaning it avoids offending anyone), attracts an audience, is clear and true. If it fails any of these tests, it's not ready for publication. Keep trying.

From Bad to Good

Here's a 2020 headline from the insurance company Generali: 'Energy Hub for Generali workers' Physical, Mental Wellness'. What's wrong with this headline? It has made all the major mistakes. There is no verb. There is no incentive to read it. What is the Energy Hub? What has Generali done? Why should the reader care?

The answer to these questions is in the first two sentences of the press release: 'Insurance company Generali revitalizes the energy of its employees by launching an "Energy Hub" project for them to promote a healthy and sustainable lifestyle. The Energy Hub, located in the Generali Tower in Milan, Italy, is dedicated to stimulate the physical and mental energy of all employees.'

These two sentences are repetitive in both words ('energy' is used four times) and concept (it's for employees), but they have the information.

A better headline would be 'Generali Opens "Energy Hub" to Promote Employee Wellness'. This way, there are two active verbs—a company that's doing something good for its employees and an explanation of what the Energy Hub is. It's got all the facts and a positive message, and piques the curiosity of the reader about what this Energy Hub is all about.

Sometimes companies try to latch on to a holiday or recent news event to get publicity. That can work well, but only if it's well timed, relevant and sensitive to the nature of the holiday.

A famous communication blunder included a mattress company that produced an ad timed for the anniversary of the 9/11 attack with two upright mattresses falling. Insensitive, that's for certain.

Face-Palm Headlines

Even journalists get headlines wrong sometimes. Here are some front-page headlines from major news sites, from boring to cringeworthy:

- 'Day's Light, Leaves Signalling Noticeable Shift to Autumn' (*Arizona Daily Star*)
- 'For Swing Voters, Tossup For President' (*Chicago Tribune*)

- 'Canadian Book-Buying Habits Haven't Changed Much in the Last Year' (*Forbes*)
- 'A Nuclear Explosion Would Be a Disaster' (*Observer*)
- 'World Bank Says Poor Need More Money' (AP)

There's Headline Help Available

If you're trying to come up with a headline that really packs a punch, try a headline generator. There are lots out there. SEO expert Neil Patel says the Content Idea Generator by Portent is best, with Topic Idea Generator by HubSpot a close second.[*]

They are not magic wands, though. Take what they generate and make sure it's succinct, conveys your message to your audience and has that special hook to draw your readers in. And make sure it doesn't overpromise on the content, spilling over into clickbait territory.

The generators certainly aren't foolproof. They are more a source of ideas for blog posts than true solutions for catchy headlines. All you do is enter a few words related to your topic—keywords, if you will—and get a suggestion for a story headline.

Enter 'headline writing' and you get:

---

[*] 'The Definitive Guide to Writing a Headline that Doesn't Suck (Tips, Tactics & Tools Included)', Neilpatel.com, https://neilpatel.com/blog/write-better-headlines/

• Why Headline Writing Is Killing You

Hopefully, after reading this chapter, writing compelling and truthful headlines won't be fatal but, rather, a fun challenge.

Exercises

Try your hand at the art of headline-writing. Remember the guidelines.

1. Edit these real-world headlines to be short, punchy and attention-grabbing. Tips: Take out all the superfluous words; add an action verb; engage your audience.
   a. Rheinmetall will equip German troops with laser duel simulators for realistic training exercises (Tip: Laser duels sound really cool but this headline doesn't)
   b. Wendy's Celebrates Breakfast Launch by Awarding Drive-Thru Customers with Free Breakfast Sandwiches for a Year (Tip: Readers only care about the free stuff)
   c. Ferrari World Abu Dhabi's Family Zone Now Open to the Public (Tip: Use a verb)

2. Write a headline for a story you'd like to tell about your company or organization. It can be a press release, a blog post or a Tweet with a link to

website content. Write twenty versions, like they do on Upworthy. Whittle the best one down to its essence and see if you can find a way to grab the reader's attention with it.

3. Go to your favourite news site and look at the top 5 headlines. Check that each one:
   a. Uses the active voice
   b. Has an action verb
   c. Is just six or seven words long

4. Look at the headline of a story you actually clicked on and read. Does it follow the TACT (Taste, Attractiveness, Clarity, Truth) rule?

3

Story Alchemy

—No One Has Time to Listen beyond the First Few Paragraphs—

Overview

Now that you've got their attention with a snappy headline, focus on crafting the beginning of a story that will keep them reading. Based on what you've read in previous chapters, you'll need to keep your mission top of mind but concentrate on your message. This is key to keeping your brand or company image consistent.

Remember who you're talking to with this particular story. Who's in the audience? Are you talking to tech-savvy entrepreneurs who might need your software, or are you explaining what you do for a living to your elderly aunt? Speak so that they can understand, engage and respond.

In this chapter, you'll learn how to write a good lead, which is a fancy journalism term for the first few paragraphs. Once you've grabbed your readers' attention with the headline, the lead needs to hold on to it. You'll do this by explaining why and providing big-picture context that your readers relate to. Lastly, we'll explain how to keep your readers engaged until the end.

Grab Them When You Can

So you've got a good headline and now you've got to reel them in with the first few sentences. Give them what they are looking for, and keep them interested enough to keep reading.

That's the definition of a good lead. Provide the key information and entice the reader to read on—all in as few words as possible. What's the key information? Easy—it's who, what, when, where, why and how.

You don't need to cram all that information into the first paragraph. What and why (as in, why the reader should care) are the most important.

Remember your audience too. Here's an example: 'To Kick Off National Breakfast Week, Kellogg's Is Giving Away Delicious High-Fibre Cereal'. That headline is mediocre. Concentrate, instead, on what's important to your readers—which is free food, of course. In that case, 'Kellogg's to Give Away Delicious High-Fibre Cereal to Celebrate National Breakfast Week' might have been better.

In the lead that follows, Kellogg's tells us that Americans don't eat enough fibre, even though they know it's healthy, and the company is going to help by giving away free cereal. That fits the bill in terms of who, what, when and why, but it's not very engaging.

It turns out a few paragraphs later that Kellogg's has its own brand-new data about Americans' breakfast habits! As we'll explain in Chapter 5, 'Using Numbers', data can give your news the authority, credibility and context that amps up its value.

This might have been a better lead:

'As many as 73 per cent of Americans say that a high-fibre breakfast is important, but just 17 per cent choose fibre-rich options, according to a survey conducted by Kellogg's. The leading breakfast food maker is giving away free high-fibre cereal during National Breakfast Week to help consumers make healthier choices.'

Unfortunately, Kellogg's left the details about how to get the free food until the end, which not only breaks the rule of answering the question 'how' as soon as possible, but also feels like a trick to get the reader to read till the end. That's not very friendly to consumers.

The 10,000-Foot View

Alongside the who-what-when-where-why-how, you need to give the readers the big picture. This is sometimes called the '10,000-foot view'. Think of it as describing what you see when you're in an airplane above the Earth. You can only see the landscape but not individual people, cars and trees. This is also called context and helps people understand why they should care.

In the Kellogg's example, the data offers the big picture—that a survey shows Americans aren't eating the healthiest breakfasts and that the company wants to help with that. The company news and the big picture are connected and relevant.

Sometimes this context is called the 'nut graph' because it's the hard centre of the story. Some news agencies, such as Bloomberg, insist that the fourth paragraph be the nut graph.

You can also start your story with the big picture, then drill down to the news. For example, the collection of stories on the UNICEF website about what it does includes one that has the following lead: 'Malaria, pneumonia, diarrhoea, HIV and tuberculosis are preventable and treatable. But they are still killing children in large numbers.'

After two paragraphs of statistics on how many children die of these each year and in what regions of the world, we read about UNICEF's response: 'These trends can be reversed. UNICEF works around the world to protect and prevent children from dying of disease. We support countries to strengthen primary healthcare systems—especially at the community level—and combat common infectious diseases.'

This story illustrates the problem (children dying), the evidence and scope (data), and the point of the story in the fourth (nut) paragraph, with the powerful sentence, 'These trends can be reversed'.

This is a refreshing approach because it's not all about the organization; it's a story about the big picture—a global problem—and the organization's efforts to rectify it.

Seal the Deal with a Quote

What does your company's CEO say about your news? Or an expert in the field? Or a well-known customer? Traditional principles of persuasion indicate that a quote from someone in authority or someone with a valued opinion not only adds a human voice to your corporate story, it also adds credibility and weight to it.

So, what's a good quote? A good quote should support the facts and at least hint at your organization's mission and the big picture, because that's what leadership is about—the mission and the big picture.

What a quote should NOT do is introduce new information. It's there to lend credibility to the news already presented. It may include some of the big picture as well.

Here's an example: 'US retailer Dick's Sporting Goods partnered with sports apparel maker Under Armour to launch a shoe designed by and for female basketball players.'

The big picture is right in the first paragraph: support for women's sports. Then comes detail on the research into the physiology of women's feet that went into the new product, citing the cooperation of three professional female basketball players.

This is followed by a quote from Dick's CEO, Lauren Hobart: 'Our hope is that this is a big step forward on the availability of women's athletic equipment, specifically designed for her.' And later, a quote by Under Armour president, North America, Stephanie Pugliese: 'This shoe was designed by a team of extraordinary women, and now we get to see incredibly talented female athletes like Bella [Alarie], Kaila [Charles] and Tyasha [Harris], wearing the shoe on the court this season.'

These are great quotes backing up the two companies' dedication to women's sports and quality products for better sports performance.

Coffee-shop chain Starbucks told a good story well with its news headline, 'Starbucks Opens Two All-Female Stores in India.'

The first paragraph had the key information—when, what and where: 'This week, Starbucks store lead Kirti Sharma and her all-female team opened a new café in the heart of Delhi, one of two new Starbucks stores in India staffed entirely by women. Sharma, the first woman in her family to enter the workforce, wants both her team and the world to know that women, "we can do anything".'

The next paragraph gave some details, the next a new quote from Sharma with a nod to the 'why' of the news: 'Times are changing in India. We have to make a change in our society. We have to start it from our homes.'

Next, the story included some statistics to support why such a move was needed, showing the 10,000-foot view: 'A 2019 report from the World Bank found that in India, only about 20 per cent of working-age women participate in the labour force.'

The remainder included more of Sharma's story of making her dream come true to have a career and how she tasted her 'destiny' when she tasted a cup of coffee. The story received a lot of press coverage—unfortunately, mostly with quotes from the CEO of Starbucks's joint venture in India, not Sharma.

The Inverted Pyramid

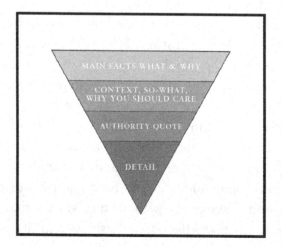

There are lots of tricks of the trade beyond who-what-when-why-how. One technique journalists use to structure their stories is the inverted pyramid.

The widest part, at the top, reminds you to put the most important information at the beginning, followed by a little more detail (for example, add the 10,000-foot view or the 'why' here), then the quote that lends authority to the story, followed by additional details, such as the 'how' (to get free cereal, for example). Both the Kellogg's and the Starbucks stories do this well.

See the exercises at the end of this chapter to try this for yourself.

Feature Stories

Feature stories are in-depth examinations of a topic and the people involved, written in a more creative way and with a different structure. They can be used to highlight a piece of news beyond the facts, delving into the why and how of a story. The best features focus on the person or the people at the heart of the news. The latter are sometimes called human-interest stories.

Here you needn't stick to the inverted pyramid structure. You can focus on the why and how, and even tell a story much like a short story or a novella does, with a plot, descriptions and characters.

Many companies, such as food giant Nestlé, have blogs and newsrooms with feature stories that look at the issues that affect their business and the world.

Many are written by employees or highlight employee expertise or activism.

Nestlé, which uses cocoa in many of its products, such as Smarties, Aero bars and Quality Street chocolates, posted a feature about the relationship between deforestation and cocoa farming.[*] While it's easy to say that cocoa farms should not cause deforestation and that thirty-three companies, including Nestlé, have committed to sourcing cocoa that does not destroy forests, it's also important to protect the livelihood of the people who work the land in and around these forests. The article describes this delicate balance and offers a possible solution that could reverse the deforestation trend.

The article doesn't start in a typical way for a company—certainly not like a press release announcing something. It says: 'The world needs forests. They are vital to maintaining biodiversity and helping combat climate change. At the same time, forests have suffered since the invention of the plough, as people have cut them down to plant crops for food and cash. The bulldozer just made things worse.'

It starts with the big picture and explains the problem. Then it drills down to the dire situation of the forests in Côte d'Ivoire and Ghana, the producers of 70 per cent of the world's cocoa, and then poses a

[*] Darrell High, 'Forests, Cocoa and Farmers', Nestle, March 2019, https://www.nestle.com/stories/protect-forests-grow-cocoa-help-farmers

question: 'How did this happen, and is cocoa to blame? If so, what is Nestlé and the industry doing about it?'

Only then does it delve into the company's cocoa-sourcing practices, plans and commitments.

This technique, and long-form or feature-writing in general, is useful for pieces meant to position your company as a thought leader in your industry or to highlight global or local issues for which your company is part of the solution.

These kind of 'think' pieces take time and research, and often the help of professional writers, but can be worth the effort in terms of long-term branding.

Start with the People

Stories about people are the most popular among storytellers because you are allowed, even encouraged, to steer away from a traditional summary lead that starts off with the what and why. You still need to hook your reader with the headline and the lead. (After all, even fiction writers need to do this.)

Here are a few common ways, with examples, to start a feature article about people that captures the attention of the readers:

- The anecdote
  When Jana arrived at the factory, there was syrup spilt everywhere. Within thirty minutes, she had it cleaned and the systems operating at full speed.

Thanks to leadership crisis training, she was prepared.

- Leading with a quote
  'Don't touch me,' she exclaimed when the man tried to hold her arm as she wobbled. The 102-year-old Maria was determined to show she was as independent as when she celebrated the eightieth anniversary of her first day at Widget Company Inc.

- Descriptive lead
  The orange sun beat down on the arid pavement. Dressed in black shorts, an orange tank top and a broad-brimmed hat, Jayden was careful to conserve her last bottle of water. She had three more kilometres to go in the summer heat, running a race to raise money for the local food bank.

- Literary, historical or lyrical allusion
  You can't always get what you want. The Rolling Stones was playing in the reception area of the IT department. Malik, the head of technology services, says those lyrics are exactly what he says to some employees who come in requesting services that don't exist yet, like a computer that never crashes.

- Punch lead
  The successor to the CEO has been named.

- Direct address
  You can save thirty minutes a day with these new tools from Sture in the IT department, our expert on these matters.

- Question lead
  What would you do if you were locked in a room and had lost your key? That's exactly what happened to Shanaya. Listen to how she got out.

- Then and now
  It took Jake two days to get there, but Emma arrived in fifteen minutes. The difference? Jake travelled in 1918 and Emma in 2018. Transportation has certainly changed.

Read more about people stories in Chapter 7, 'Keeping It Human'.

Q&As

You can also tell your story in the form of interview questions and answers, also known as a Q&A. Such articles are usually edited for length and clarity. Writing Q&As are easy and fun. They go like this:

Q: How do you write a Q&A?
A: Simple. Write a headline and introductory sentence setting the scene, with the who, where, when and why of the interview. Then write out the questions and

answers that show the elements of the interview. Use the most interesting questions and answers, and if you edit them, be sure to not change the meaning too much, since the interviewee's words are not yours to change. Don't add any narrative.

Q: Is it really that simple?
A: Yes. It's basically a transcript of an interview, cleaned up for grammar and often shortened to include the most relevant parts of the discussion.

Q: Where can I learn more about interviewing?
A: Go to Chapter 7, 'Keeping It Human', to learn more about interviewing and engaging people.

The more popular a person is, such as the CEO of a company, the more suited the Q&A format is for an article. It's for when a reader wants to hang on to the interviewee's every word.

The Listicle, aka Top Tips or Best Lists

Another way to present your story is with a listicle, which we mentioned in Chapter 2, 'Killer Headlines'. BuzzFeed is often cited as having invented this type of story, with headlines that tend to get a lot of clicks.

Why do they tend to get clicks? Well, people love to make lists and read lists. They are a way to organize information in a digestible way, which we sorely need in an era of information overload. Lists simplify and categorize, which is exactly what our brains crave when they encounter new information. Listicles also offer solutions to a problem—another reason they are enjoyable to read and share.

The lists that may come from people you interview are often tips, but they can also be the rankings of best experiences, products, ideas, locations and more. The format is easy. It goes something like this:

Headline: 7 tips for writing awesome people stories

Lead: Ever wonder how to write a great list-article? Wonder no more, here are seven top tips from experts around the world.

Body:

1. Top tips are listed in numerical order.
2. Use them when the person you interview is offering great advice.
3. Odd-numbered lists are more popular than even-numbered lists.
4. List 5 or 7 tips or 17, but not 8 or 12.
5. Include a headline and an introductory sentence to explain what is coming.

Writing for SEO

As we explained in Chapter 2, 'Killer Headlines', you need to keep SEO in mind when you're writing. Because no matter how well you write, it's important that your content pops up in the Google, Bing or Yahoo search results so it gets read. SEO is about making sure your content gets seen.

It's not easy, since Google changes the algorithm eight times a day on average, according to SEO expert Neil Patel. Ideally, with SEO, you'll get your content to the top of the list. Competition is stiff, so you may want to target the first page of results, because that makes a difference too. A full 91.5 per cent of clicks come from the first page of results. If your story is on page two, you're competing for just 4.8 per cent of the total clicks on that keyword.*

However, if you know the basics of keyword search and meta descriptions, you'll be on your way to optimizing. You'll also be better prepared to decide whether you need to hire an SEO specialist or agency.

Keywords, as we've said, are words we all type into the search bar when we want to find information, buy something or find a specific website. Ideally, you want to match your content to the words your audience might type in.

For example, someone planning a holiday might type in 'Spain travel' if they want more information, 'book Madrid hotel' if they're ready to reserve or

---

* Jessica Lee, 'No. 1 Position in Google Gets 33% of Search Traffic [Study]', Search Engine Watch, 20 June 2013, https://www.searchenginewatch.com/2013/06/20/no-1-position-in-google-gets-33-of-search-traffic-study/

'Madrid Hilton' if they want a specific website. So, if you indeed own a hotel in Madrid, you would want those words to be somewhere at the top of your story, and some in the headline. SEO research can also help you find out whether people are more likely to type 'Spain travel' or 'Spain holiday' into the search bar.

SEO is much more than the headline. Meta descriptions, for example, play a big role in search results. In case you're unfamiliar with the term, a meta description is the snippet of information below the link of a search result. Its purpose is to describe the contents of the page to the searcher. The end goal is to convince and persuade the searcher to click through to your website. These should be up to 160 characters in length and no more. Otherwise, they'll be cut off.

Here's an example. When you google Lonely Planet, you get a small box:

www.lonelyplanet.com
Lonely Planet / Travel Guides & Travel Information
Love travel? Discover, plan and book your perfect trip with expert advice, travel guides, destination information and inspiration from Lonely Planet.

The main headline tells you what Lonely Planet does: It's a source of travel guides and information. The meta-description below asks a question: 'Love travel?' If you're searching for travel info, you probably love to travel, so you're going to read on. The rest tells you exactly what you can do via Lonely Planet—'Discover, plan and book your perfect trip'—and what you'll get from them—'expert advice . . . inspiration', etc.

That says it all. There are four active verbs in the first six words. That motivates people to act! It's got the keywords 'travel', 'book', 'trip' and 'guide', which people who want to go on a holiday are probably using. It gives you a reason to click on the link. All in 128 characters.

Exercises

1. Here are some facts of a story. Write a lead in as few words as possible (try to limit the paragraph to 40 words). Include only the most important facts.

   a. A bakery starts selling bagel burgers.

   b. The bakery is in Littletown.

   c. The bakery is family-owned.

   d. Littletown has a small business-loan programme that Little Town Bagels used to develop its new product.

   e. The bakery is called Little Town Bagels.

   f. Littletown doesn't have any other bagel shop.

   g. The bakery is 100 years old.

   h. Little Town Bagels is teaming up with a nearby ketchup and mustard factory to secure condiments.

   i. Littletown has a population of 10,000.

   j. Mayor Sally Sue Porchlight said, 'I love Little Town Bagels. I'm going to get me a bagel burger as soon as I can.'

k. The bagel burgers will be on sale from 1 April.
l. There will be a veggie version.

2. Here is a famous lead from a 1968 *New York Times* story. Review the who-what-where-when-how and see what journalist Mark Hawthorne included, how much was packed into this one sentence and what he left to the second sentence to prompt readers to read on.

'A 17-year-old boy chased his pet squirrel up a tree in Washington Square Park yesterday afternoon, touching off a series of incidents, in which 22 persons were arrested and eight persons, including five policemen, were injured.'

3. SEO practice: Type in the first word or two of something relevant to your business. For example, you own an organic food store in Singapore. Type 'Singapore organic' into Google, and don't press Enter—just see how Google autocompletes the search. Those are the things that people have tended to search for recently, related to 'Singapore' and 'organic'. These are the first clues about the keywords you should use in stories and other web content in order for them to pop up in Google searches. Now write a meta-description for your company (155 characters or less) that includes those keywords and others that may be important to you, such as 'delivery' or one of your speciality products.

4

Seeing Is Believing
—Visual Helpers—

Overview

In this chapter, you will learn how images boost audience attention and memory. It will explain why visuals are necessary and what happens when you go without them.

You will explore the types of images that can be created to accompany and amplify your story. The chapter will address guidelines for choosing videos, photos or other images and explain what is needed, when and why. It will also introduce you to infographics that can be used instead of heavy data, or numbers, and show you some examples.

The chapter will be a window into what may be involved when you choose visuals, so you can work quickly and efficiently with professionals who know the ins and outs of the medium.

Visuals Make a Message Understandable

We don't even think about it, but we prefer pictures to words. Why? Because we need less time to process them and we retain their meaning longer. In fact, we process them 60,000 times faster than text. This figure is widely attributed to research by 3M, the company that makes Post-It notes. Another way to look at it is through the lens of historical context. We've been communicating with images for more than 30,000 years, but writing didn't begin until around 3000 BC.*

Consider this real-life scenario. How long does it take for you to understand this image on the right versus the text on the left?

Which one do you understand faster?

---

* Ewan Clayton, 'Where did writing begin?', British Library, https://www.bl.uk/history-of-writing/articles/where-did-writing-begin#

Even if the image just had the text 'No U-Turn' without any visual, it would still take longer to understand and you would be less likely to remember it than the simple image. A review of fifty-five experiments showed an overwhelming increase in our likelihood to succeed, following instructions with illustrations versus those without.[*]

Consider the weather. That's something we ask about every day. Imagine a weather app without images. A single picture can explain partly cloudy with some rain in the east of a country in the morning. It takes many words to do the same.

Think of images as a key asset to boost your narrative. Humans put images directly into their long-term memory and can process multiple pictures at once. Text goes into the short-term memory one word at a time before it is processed into long-term memory. This is why people competing in memory contests use patterns of mental images to help them win. For example, champions remember hundreds of numbers by placing them in an imaginary house with multiple rooms with people and objects. The images trigger associations to help remember patterns and numbers, as described in the book *Moonwalking with Einstein* by Joshua Foer.[†]

---

[*] W. Howard Levie and Richard Lentz, 'Effects of text illustrations: A review of research', *Educational Technology Research and Development*, December 1982, https://link.springer.com/article/10.1007/BF02765184

[†] Joshua Foer, *Moonwalking with Einstein: The Art and Science of Remembering Everything*, Penguin Books, 2012.

Visuals Make a Message Persuasive and Believable

A study at The Wharton School gave the same presentation to two groups of people. In the first group, there were no visuals to accompany the presentation—and 50 per cent of the audience found it persuasive. The second group watched the same presentation, but with visuals—and 67 per cent of them found it persuasive.

Images will increase your clickability and discoverability in Google searches. Beyond that, when presented with a picture in addition to text or even an audio presentation, people will remember up to 65 per cent of the information. If there's no picture, they only remember 10 per cent, according to a round-up of research by Hubspot. That's definitely a good case for adding an image.[*]

Not only does an image help your audience understand faster, remember more and decide to click through to your content, but images also make your text more believable. A study at Colorado State University showed that by simply adding a picture of a brain to the results of the neuroscience study, readers found the study more credible.

---

[*] Jesse Mawhinney, '50 Visual Content Marketing Statistics You Should Know in 2021', Hubspot, https://blog.hubspot.com/marketing/visual-content-marketing-strategy

Use Visuals to Show Authority

We believe something is effective if a professional tells us it is. This links directly back to the use of authority in persuasion techniques. Authority is something that can be visualized. What's better than saying nine out of ten doctors recommend this toothpaste? It's better to show it with images of doctors.

Look at all the advertisements that promote medications or toothpaste. Usually, the actors wear white coats to look like doctors or dentists, when, in reality, they have never even set foot in medical school.

Visuals to Share

By creating visuals and giving permission to share, you increase your chances of reaching more of your target audience. You're making it easier and more attractive to share your story via social media and easier for journalists to write about it.

Sharing means making the images downloadable, in multiple formats when possible, along with instruction for private and commercial use. If you get your brand into the image, sharing becomes a free advertising opportunity too.

Not only are news editors much more likely to choose stories for publication if there is a visual with it, but search engines are also programmed to prioritize content that contains optimized images. (Images, like other content, can be optimized for SEO too.) Here are a few types of visuals you can create and share to boost the chances of your story getting picked up in the news or your name sticking with the visual as the creator of the content.

Infographics

There are ways to show something via an image even if there isn't a lot of data behind it. These tend to revolve around process, structure, flow and change. The most common event is an organizational change. Someone is hired or fired and that event instigates a reshuffling of people. Writing about how Team B will now be reporting to Team C, with sub-groups sorted by product and not region, is hard to write about. A before and after organizational chart makes it so much easier.

Any time you are telling a story that involves process, structure, a timeline or a location, you might want to consider creating infographics. It's important to realize you can create an infographic without much data. If you do have a nice set of data, you can read about data visualization in storytelling in Chapter 5, 'Using Numbers'.

For example, if you make diapers and support sustainability, you might want to create an infographic that shows where the raw materials come from. Not everyone knows that trees are actually a key ingredient. This way, an infographic that shows the replanting of the forests your company uses for raw materials shows your commitment to sustainability and informs the customer in an instant. You can share the infographic with news outlets for when they write about your company or about forest fires or climate change. This will get your name into the news.

Infographics and charts can be made in PowerPoint, Excel, Google Docs and/or Apple products. There are also online services that are partially free and simple, such as Canva or Piktochart. In the next chapter, where heavy data is involved, you may need more complex tools, from Tableau and Microsoft's Power BI to Adobe's Creative Suite.

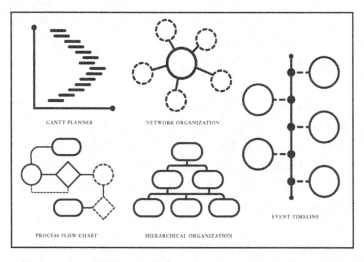

Ways to visualize actions or events

Here's a list of examples of simple infographics that don't require large amounts of data but illustrate a point well:

a. **Flow charts:** Flow charts are best used to show processes. A process can be how a product is made, such as tracking the tomato in your salad from seed to farm to store to table. A process may be instructional, also known as a how-to. It's not easy to replace the blade of a lawnmower without a step-by-step how-to visual instruction. A process can even be something in your head, such as the thought process we go through before making a consumer decision to purchase something.

b. **Timelines:** Timelines are similar to flow charts but progress on a schedule. They are great for showing major events in the life of a person, company or country. They are also useful to show the timeline of something simple like a product launch or an advertising campaign.

Speaking of product launches, timelines may also be used for planning. These are also known as Gantt charts, a type of bar chart named after its inventor Henry Gantt. Gantt charts are more often used inside a company for planning than outside it for communication with the public.

c. **Organizational charts and Venn diagrams:** These are both used to show relationships. The organizational chart shows a more linear display of something, such as who reports to whom. The Venn diagram shows interdependent relationships, or where things overlap.

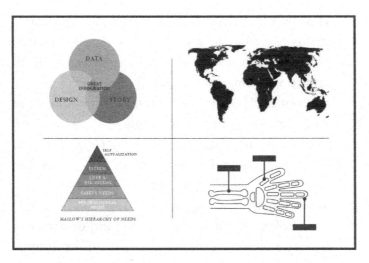

Examples of visuals used to explain complex concepts: Venn diagram, maps, hierarchy pyramids and anatomical designs

d. **Informational and list infographics:** These are infographics that group things together to allow for deeper insight. There is no process to them, nor is there a timeline.

They may also be checklists, to-do lists, suggestion lists or information required to perform a task. 'The top 10 destinations in Sao Paulo for tourists' or 'Seven things to do to stay healthy in a pandemic' are both examples of information presented as lists.

e. **Hierarchical diagrams:** While the organizational chart can also be seen as a hierarchical chart, there are other things that can be presented in order of importance that aren't about reporting lines.

Maslow's hierarchy of needs is a well-known one. In this book, we've also talked about the inverted pyramid for news-writing and the hierarchy from data to wisdom.

f. **Anatomical:** When the internal functioning of something is difficult to explain in words, an anatomical infographic is the way to go. Anyone who's put together a piece of IKEA furniture has used a list of anatomical pictures to get there.

g. **Maps:** Finally, there are maps. Maps can be simple or complex, depending on the amount of data you use. The cholera example below is quite simple. It placed the addresses of deaths on a map with dots. Mapping tools have advanced rapidly and today you can easily plot out data on a map using PowerPoint or any of the simple tools mentioned above.

A map that shows the routes of an airline is a 'flow map.' John Snow's well-known cholera death map created in the 1850s was a 'dot map'. Maps that are 3D are 'prism maps'. 'Isarithmic maps' show spatial surfaces and are often used to show weather patterns in precipitation or heat. Choropleth maps use colour to shade distinct areas. These are often used to show differences in area population, from wealth to voting trends, or the countries in which a company or organization is active.

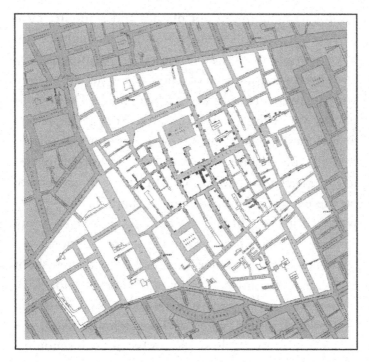

This map was created by John Snow in 1854. He plotted the cholera outbreak in London so its source could be visually identified to a single infected water pump. He showed something that couldn't be seen in words or numbers only.

Pictures

The first photograph was taken about 175 years ago. In contrast, it was estimated that in 2020 alone, a trillion photos were taken.[*] Additionally, we have 7.4 trillion

---

[*] 'How Many Photos Will Be Taken in 2020?', Mylio.com, 10 January 2020, https://focus.mylio.com/tech-today/how-many-photos-will-be-taken-in-2020

photos hanging out in our phones and computer hard drives. Yet, we still seem to not have enough, or not have the right one for a new story. Preparation is key.

There are a number of photos you should have in your archives, labelled and easily searchable. The obvious photos are of the CEO, leaders and your headquarters or factories. The less obvious, and more fun, are photos that fit your themes. So, if you make kitchen ovens, it'd be prudent to have plenty of pictures of good food, people eating and even recipes to share. Have pictures where your ovens fit multiple holidays. It is an easy way to place your product and build brand association.

When you have your leaders booked for a photoshoot (and we do recommend hiring a professional for this), take many pictures for unexpected messages. If you only take pictures of your CEO happy and smiling, you won't be able to use those photos when she is sending a message in a crisis or has negative news.

When preparing photos, find a format guide online so that you choose the right one for the right channel, depending on what is in the photo. The formats (file extensions) include .psd, .pdf, .svg, .png, .jpeg, .tiff, .ai and .gif.

Once you have your format selected, think about your photo's display and size. Portrait or landscape? What is your aspect ratio? And your pixel size? For example, if you need a new cover photo for your Facebook page, the photo needs to be 851 x 479 pixels, whereas a profile photo for Twitter is 400 x 400.

(Your favourite photo may not work, as you may have experienced in your personal social media channels.) Here are some of the preset options you can use in Adobe Spark just to create a social media post. Canva, for example, has many templates for all social media, presentations materials, print materials and pictures. Each requires special formatting.

Luckily, there are photo- and video-processing experts who do formatting quickly and efficiently. Their job looks easy but is actually quite challenging. When 85 per cent of adults view images and content on multiple devices at the same time, it's critical to deliver them in the right formats.

Good pictures in multiple formats are hard to come by. Newsrooms spend a lot of time searching for the right photo and more time cropping it to their preferred size. Once you know your message, you should take the time to have photos available and shared.

Videos

Preparing videos is also important. See our separate chapter about creating video content and selecting channels for it.

Don't Forget the Labels

Whatever visual you are using, do not forget the importance of labels. For photos, it's the headlines and/or captions. For videos, it's the title and the subtitles. For infographics and charts, it's about the headline and in-chart labelling.

The text needs to be simple and clear. The sourcing needs to be transparent. The fonts need to be readable.

Chapters 2 and 3 on writing headlines and context should have you ready to handle your labels like a pro.

Exercises

1. Create a presentation. Make two versions. Add visual prompts to one and none to the other. Present to two groups and survey their impressions after. Compare.
2. Create a social media post about something you did this weekend. Send one with a picture and one without. Which is the more popular?
3. Create a guide for photo and video sizes you will need to promote a product of your choice across social media. How can you create these? Which tools will you use?
4. Call your local TV station or newspaper, and ask them what formats they require for pictures and videos.
5. You are about to launch a new product. It is a small machine that scoops up your dog's poo for you and puts it in a bag for the trash bin without you having to touch it or clean it after. Sketch four infographics you could create to explain what this is.

6. Find two news items on corporate websites (they are usually on a page called 'newsroom' on the main web page) that are lacking a photo or are using boring images. Find two replacements for each. Explain why your images would be better than what the websites have used.

Do You Need These Visuals? A Checklist

Photos

- Is your concept hard to remember?
- Is your message better relayed by showing a colour, an action or some other representation?
- Is your audience more likely to respond to a picture?
- Is your message 100 per cent text?

Videos (see more about video in later chapters)

- Can your message wait for the weeks required to produce the video?
- Is your message so complex that your audience needs to see it in action?
- Will seeing your message in action boost interest?

Charts

- Is there data?
- If the answer is yes, move on to the next chapter.

5

Using Numbers

—Data Is Your Friend—

Overview

As we've described in the previous chapter, one of the classic methods of persuasion is to use the impression of authority to promote your product or message. Authority doesn't have to come from a person. Data, and the analysis and presentation of data, give the same effect—boosting credibility.

For many, just the mention of data gives the impression of being factual and accurate. That's because they equate data with facts. Facts are, by definition, accurate, making them compelling and persuasive. So, data adds accuracy to your story while making it more compelling and persuasive.

Data helps show changes, trends and comparisons— all key ingredients for news. When things stay the same, people aren't interested. Nothing is happening. But with data, there is always a way to show change and context. And with data comes the opportunity to create charts and graphs, often more sophisticated images than simple infographics. We'll discuss your options here and how to choose the right way to illustrate your point.

This chapter will explain how you can use data to bolster the delivery of your message. It can be argued that data can be manipulated to lie and mislead. While that may be correct in some cases, it is not the rule but rather the exception. Data remains crucial for believability and persuasion.

The chapter will finish by offering some concrete tips for including numbers in narratives as well as tips for avoiding mistakes that would make your data-driven story be called out as fake news.

Data Boosts Believability

'In God we trust, the rest bring data.' This quote, attributed to W. Edwards Deming, the electrical engineer who helped develop sampling techniques used by the US Federal Census Bureau, shows how much we rely on data for decision-making.

Deming pioneered the concept of quality control in industry, using data to monitor and improve processes, and help drive the rebuilding of industry in Japan after the Second World War.

His quote embraces what modern society has learnt to believe—that data will bring us closer to the truth. Those who show data to support their statements will have a more reliable argument than those who do not. As Swedish physician Hans Rosling said to a journalist in Denmark who was trying to debate the state of countries in Africa: 'I use normal statistics from the World Bank. This is not controversial. This is not up for discussion. I am right and you are wrong.'*

Think about how you use data at work. No performance reviews are conducted without data. No bonuses are paid without data. No new products are developed without data. No divisions are shut down without data. So, why should someone buy your product without data?

Naturally, data doesn't work magic on its own. People are much more likely to remember a story than a set of statistics. Data is a tool that helps engage, enhance or explain something in your story.

Data and narrative together help explain something, while adding visuals can help engage and enlighten. Visuals with a narrative help engage readers, like we might see in a children's book, while adding data takes it to a different level to help explain a concept. The most

---

* 'Hans Rosling: Don't Use News Media to Understand the World (English Subtitles)', YouTube, 4 September 2015, https://www.youtube.com/watch?v=xYnpJGaMiXo

powerful storytelling pools all three elements together. Achieve that and you have a powerful corporate story.

This can also be seen as a modern way to look at Aristotle's *Rhetoric*. The ancient Greek philosopher said there are three kinds of persuasion—ethos, logos and pathos. Ethos is all about who you are or appear to be (remember the actor in the doctor's white coat?). It's about the reputation of your company and its leaders. Pathos is about stirring emotions, and is often used by companies, charities and goodwill operations. Logos is about logical argument and includes using data and statistics as types of reasoning.

Don't Worry, Data Doesn't Bite

You might be apprehensive about using data. Some call that mathematical anxiety. Yes, it's a thing. In the 1950s, a researcher labelled it 'mathemaphobia'. It is tension or apprehension about one's ability to do maths.[*] In one survey, about 93 per cent of adults in the US have some sort of maths anxiety and almost a fifth deal with high levels of anxiety.[†]

---

[*] Mark H. Ashcraft, 'Math Anxiety: Personal, Educational, and Cognitive Consequences', Sage Journals, 1 October 2002, https://journals.sagepub.com/doi/10.1111/1467-8721.00196

[†] Christie Blazer, 'Strategies for Reducing Math Anxiety. Information Capsule. Volume 1102', ERIC, September 2011, https://eric.ed.gov/?id=ED536509

This means that almost everyone has some degree of trouble with maths and might not want to work with data. But fears are often a product of unfamiliarity. Certainly, the rise of the calculator and its inclusion in a phone we carry everywhere make us less likely to do maths in our heads. Want to see the final price of a gadget that's on sale at 35 per cent off? Whip out your phone calculator, or ask Alexa or Siri. The ease at which we can do maths on our phones means we aren't doing it in our heads. It's not that we can't—it's just that we've gotten rusty because we haven't had to. This may compound anxieties about numbers and data.

That means we're even more impressed by those who can do maths for us, especially those who can present statistical data. We tend to believe it is all true, rather than do the calculations ourselves to be able to challenge the numbers. How many of you actually went to the footnoted source of the survey cited above to check its validity?

Speaking of challenging the numbers, take a look at this 'solution' to poverty. It went viral on social media one year when the lottery jackpot was particularly high. The social media card said:

Lottery Jackpot: $1.3 Billion
U.S. Population> 300 Million
If we share it, everyone gets $4.33 million
each and we solve poverty!

Take a moment to do the maths (yes, you can do it).

It works out to $4.33 per person, not $4.33 million, doesn't it? That may buy every American a Big Mac, but it won't solve poverty. Still, the post got millions of shares.

Now that you have a healthy scepticism about data and have reaffirmed your ability to do some simple maths, it's time to see how you can use data in your storytelling. In fact, everyone's rustiness with maths is a great opportunity for you to swoop in and wow readers with your data. Here are some ways to select and gather data to amplify your story.

Readers Hate to Do the Maths

We just asked you to do the maths to show how many people don't—because they can't or don't want to. So, in your communications, make sure your readers don't have to do the maths at all. How? By being transparent and sure of your numbers.

Be aware of two common mistakes made by people who have embraced data. The first is putting too many numbers into your content. The second is forcing the reader to do the maths in their heads. They tend to show up together. We'll address both here.

Sometimes we get too close to our data and want to put everything into the story or content being created. Doing this risks a number overload. Many of us struggle to remember a few PIN codes or passwords, so asking an audience to remember many numbers is a tall order.

For most content, especially online content and emails, it's better to show headline numbers as numerals than text, according to leading user-experience researcher Nielsen Norman Group:

> Why do users fixate on numerals? Because numbers represent facts, which is something users typically relish. Sometimes people are looking for specific facts, such as a product's weight or size, so product pages are certainly one place where you should write numbers as numerals. But even when a number doesn't represent a product attribute, it's a more compact (and thus attractive) representation of hard information than flowery verbiage.[*]

So numbers get noticed, but if you put too many in one sentence or paragraph, you deplete their value by turning them into a commodity. Select one main number to anchor your story and use that early on. Add a few key numbers that support the main one. Put everything else in a table at the bottom.

By disciplining your storytelling to select a key number to start with, you won't fall into the second trap

---

[*] Jakob Nielsen, 'Show Numbers as Numerals When Writing for Online Readers', Nielsen Norman Group, 15 April 2007, https://www.nngroup.com/articles/web-writing-show-numbers-as-numerals/

of making the reader do the maths. If you tell readers that profit rose from $45 to $55, and the number of employees fell from 2000 to 1800, while sales changed from $2000 to $2200, they will struggle to read the sentence. That sentence has six numbers and twenty digits going three different directions. You're asking them to do the maths in their heads as they read. But what is more likely to happen is that they will stop reading.

How can you fix this? You can just as easily say profit rose 22 per cent, helped by investments and outstripping sales growth. That doesn't mean you should obscure the rest of the numbers. Transparency is still a valuable element. Just put them in a table at the bottom for reference, allowing you to pull out the main trends you want to convey in your story.

A note on percentages while we are here. Once you get past 100 per cent, it's better to describe the change as doubling or trebling. Telling someone something rose 200 per cent when the number rose from 2 to 6 can be confusing, Simply stating the amount trebled is easier to digest.

Boggle with Big Numbers

When using numbers so big that they boggle the mind, try to find different ways to measure the number to provide context easily identifiable by the audience.

India's national debt is about $1.6 trillion. That's a big number. What does it mean to a reader who might never save even a million in their lifetime? Context is important. There are two ways to do this. One is to offer comparisons. 'US debt is $28 trillion and China's debt is $3.2 trillion.'[*] The second way is to measure the money in spending terms. 'How many jumbo jets can you buy with a trillion dollars?'

What Is One Trillion Dollars?

A trillion is a 1 with 12 zeros after it. You can also measure a big number in physical terms. Stack up a trillion dollar bills and they'll stretch over a thousand kilometres into the air, or more than double the distance to the International Space Station.[†]

Here's another way to put it. If you earned $50,000 a year and saved all of it, it would take 20 million years to save a trillion dollars. Bill Gates, one of the richest people in the world, isn't even close to a trillion yet—though at a worth of $110 billion, he's a lot closer than most of us.

Most of these calculations come from a website called Thecalculatorsite.com. There are many out there like this one that can help you find good context for your big numbers.

---

[*] https://www.ceicdata.com/en/indicator/india/national-government-debt

[†] Becky Kleanthous, 'How Much Is a TRILLION?', The Calculator Site, 15 February 2021, https://www.thecalculatorsite.com/articles/finance/how-much-is-a-trillion.php

Rich Sources for Data

But what if you don't have a big number? Where can data be discovered? Your data can be self-generated or come from an external source. For company-generated data, look beyond your financials. You can make a data point from almost anything you do—be it production in your factory or ingredients in your products.

There are a number of rich resources for data. Here are a few below. Remember that almost every government agency in the world, from the US Federal Reserve to the Statistics Office of Finland, has an impressive array of data available free of charge.

Here are some of our favourite data sources:

- Census of India
- Pew Research
- United Nations
- European Union
- OECD
- WHO
- Gapminder
- Google Scholar
- Amazon Public Data
- Kaggle Datasets
- Subreddit
- Qlik DataMarket
- Enigma Public
- World Bank

- UNICEF
- Search the World
- Statista

You can deep-dive into data on a whole range of subjects from the weather, water contamination and air quality to literacy and vaccination rates. According to estimates by Live-counter.com, a website that measures Internet data in real-time, we'll have 40 zettabytes of data on the Internet by the end of 2020. You need to add 21 zeros to a number to get a zettabyte. With 4.4 billion Internet users, there's not much you can't get data on—from cute kittens to coal reserves. (In case you were wondering, there are 600 million kittens in the world, all of whom are presumably cute, and 1.1 trillion tonnes of proven coal reserves, according to Google search results in 2020.)

Still can't find what you need? No problem. You can always produce data by creating and conducting surveys and questionnaires.

Use a survey to ask if companies should pay higher taxes and your answers become data. Fifty per cent say yes. Twenty per cent say no and 30 per cent say they have no opinion. That's data which can be turned into a visual pie chart and used in a story.

Data Bias? Ask Who's Paying

Companies also sponsor research to obtain data that supports their message. The tobacco industry showed just how deep this approach could be taken in the 1980s and the 1990s. They sponsored research and published it as independent research. They even created 'health' magazines that were friendly to smoking.

So the next time you read about whether eggs, milk or aspirin is good (or bad) for you, look at who paid for that research.

For this book, however, we're going to assume we are working with data that carries no intentional or malicious bias. Remember the company that did research showing people are more likely to take their pet to the vet than go to the doctor themselves? As we said in Chapter 1, 'Your Message', this was a great and honest way to draw attention to the company, which helped consumers choose healthcare insurance for themselves, not their pets. If you think your company might want to commission research, you can read more about how to do that in Chapter 11, 'Sponsoring Content'.

If You Can Measure It, You Can Find Data

You can find data in just about anything to create curious information to draw attention to your company, product or message. And the data you find can spark stories and narratives. Once you start looking, it's hard to stop.

For example, walk down a city street. Look around. How many bricks are in a block of the sidewalk? How long did it take to build? How many people worked on building it? Who were those people? How long do the bricks last, on average? What is the composition of the material used to make them?

What about the residents along the street? The stores? The restaurants? How many visitors do they have? Or customers? How many meals are served in a week? How many French fries are eaten? Which week is the busiest? Which hour of the day?

The list goes on. If you can count things and sort things into categories, you can measure and compare them. That's data. Now take your product and try to apply this way of brainstorming about data to it. Or to the location of a factory. The location of your staff. Their nationalities. Your customers. Changes in any of your trends. It is all measurable. Once you've measured this, you need to start climbing the data pyramid.

The data pyramid starts with data. From there, you can sort it to create information. After that, you can analyse it to create knowledge. Then by applying it to decision/making you get wisdom. Data – information – knowledge – wisdom.

Data Analysis Leads to Storytelling

Data in itself isn't very interesting or understandable. You need to organize it and present it in a manner that turns data into information, then knowledge and then hopefully wisdom for your audience.

Here are some things to think about when preparing to present data:

- Are you highlighting a single big number?
- Are you showing a trend?
- Are you comparing two or more things?
- Are you showing relationships?
- Are you showing a process?
- Are you looking at absolute numbers or change over time?
- What is your superlative? Highest, biggest, smallest, fastest, longest?
- What part of the data do you want your audience to remember the most?

Asking yourself these questions will help keep your data simple and focused. Just like with the story elements in the first section of this book, having too many numbers or too many data sets can be confusing. Sometimes, just one number is enough. For example, it takes a factory worker seventy-five years to earn what their CEO makes in a single year.

The answer to these questions will also help you decide how to visualize the data so you can share it. For example, if you are showing a comparison of rainfall in three cities, you don't want a pie chart. A pie chart shows you parts of a whole and needs to equal 100 per cent. It's impossible to display a comparison of separate things inside a single pie chart.

The Joy of Choosing Charts

It's not unusual for someone in a communications strategy meeting to suggest creating a chart or data visualization to amplify the message. The intention is good. Remember everything we talked about regarding credibility and memorability? Execution is harder. Creating a chart requires knowledge about data and the options for each type.

Let's look at a few popular chart types:

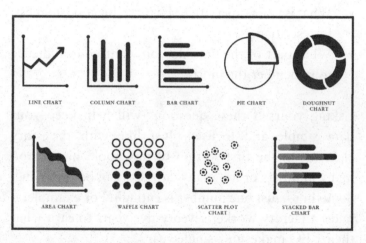

Some popular chart types

There are many excellent resources when it comes to reading about, building and selecting charts. One of our favourites is https://www.visualisingdata.com

We find ourselves returning to the 'Resources' tab time and again. Andy Kirk explains that he 'launched Visualisingdata.com to continue the process of discovery and to chart the course of the increasing popularity of the subject'. The list of organizations, institutions and companies he has worked with is vast and impressive, giving him an amazingly broad view on data visualization in all corners of the world.

Before you start shouting that you want a bar chart or a scatter plot, consider your data, as discussed above. Think about how each type of chart might help or hurt your data.

If you want to show parts of a whole, a 100 per cent stacked bar chart or a tree map chart might do the trick. But these won't ever be able to show change over time in a single snapshot. To show change over time, choose line charts or column charts.

Understanding what you want to show—trends, distribution, relationships or comparisons—is what will help set you off in the right direction.

Take waffle charts, for example. This chart is usually areas set up in stacked rows of 10x10. They are used to show pieces of a whole, often with the parts designated by shape and/or colour. Going back to our big-number example, the debt of a country per capita may be a single big number. But it can also be part of a whole if you can place it in context. India's debt is also part of world debt, and, as such, could be displayed in a waffle chart while also giving perspective and context.

Here's an overview of the most popular charts and when you might use them:

- Line chart: Use this to show change in one variable over time for each line.
- Bar chart: Use this to compare categories, such as answers to a survey.
- Column chart: Use this to show trends over time while comparing variables.
- Pie chart: Use this to show parts of a whole.
- Stacked bar chart: Use this to compare variables within whole entities. It can be simple-stacked or 100 per cent stacked, depending on the data.
- Scatter plot chart: Use this to compare relationships between two sets of data.

Chart-Making Tools

All the creation tools mentioned in the chapter on images can make data visualizations, starting with your basic PowerPoint and Excel programme in Windows to the counterparts offered by Google and Apple.

On top of that, there are dozens of apps and websites offered that specialize in chart-building, from Infogram and Piktochart to Canva and Visme. For heavy data manipulations, there are Tableau, Power BI, Adobe Creative Suite and QlikView, among others. Programmers may turn to Python, R, Java or SQL. You don't have to know this in depth as a communications specialist, but if you can speak the language of the data scientist and understand how they work, you'll be a better partner to them in creating superior data visualization, or a 'data viz' experience.

The best data scientists and programmers can work with motion and animated visualizations. The organization Gapminder, founded by Hans Rosling, helped bring such animated analysis to the general public. Rosling's mission was to bust your built-in hidden biases with his visual analysis, which he wrote about in the book *Factfulness*.*

If you want to explore how various charts are made using different creation tools or just see examples, go to the Chartmaker Directory at http://chartmaker. visualisingdata.com/

It catalogues examples and tools that help you understand which tool you need to make certain charts. The directory is crowd-sourced and always evolving. Also, check out the Gapminder website. It offers an environment for exploring the creation of public data that is quite enjoyable.

Share to Engage

Creating a chart or graph around your data and making it shareable is a good way to get attention.

Having just read about formats and sizes in the chapter on images, you may want to create the charts

---

* Hans Rosling, *Factfulness: Ten Reasons We're Wrong about the World—and Why Things Are Better Than You Think*, Sceptre, 2018.

and graphics on your own to be used by the media or other channels for your intended audience. Most smaller channels and news agencies will be grateful. The more staff-strapped they are, the more grateful they will be. This is particularly true for regional and local organizations in print and online, as well as single-operation social media channels.

However, some bigger news outlets will want to create their own with their in-house tools and style guidelines. In these cases, deliver what you have created to give inspiration, and also include a file with the raw data. If you have a survey, provide information about who was surveyed and what questions were asked. If someone else gathered the data, provide information on them.

It's always important to provide transparency in your data by linking it to your source or offering to share the spreadsheet if you own the data.

Post the data on your website with clear rules for use and attribution. Share your data with traditional news sites for when they need to create 'news' on slow news days.

Avoid Being Fake News

There are a number of ways to make data tell misleading stories. Sometimes that happens accidentally through mistakes or bias. Here are a few tips on how to avoid appearing as fake news.

1. Avoid starting the x and y axes with anything but zero.
2. Be transparent about your sources.
3. Check your research for hidden bias. The tobacco companies were paying for research and that research was flawed. The findings were biased.
4. Make sure you are showing the right amount of history and are measuring the right thing.

Corporations and Data

There are many people considered to be thought leaders in the field of data visualization. There's one, however, we should pay attention to in the area of corporate and organizational data. Willard Brinton published his book *Graphic Methods for Presenting Facts* in 1914.* It's arguably the first complete book on visualizing data for business. Investor relations communicators around the world follow principles set by him and use charts defined by him even today, possibly without even knowing it.

His book is considered to be in the public domain and is free to download. Reading it is a sobering reminder of how many principles in this field don't change. You can download the PDF here: https://aviz.fr/wiki/uploads/Bertifier/brinton-graphicMethods-1914.pdf

---

* Willard Brinton, *Graphic Methods for Presenting Facts*, BiblioLife, 2009.

His book contains a 'Principle of Expressiveness' on data that is simple and applies to not just data but perhaps all forms of communication: '*Say what you need to. No more. No less. Don't mislead.*' He combines that with a Principle of Effectiveness:' *Use the best method available to show your data.*'

The combination will help you achieve excellent messaging. It's straightforward, sage advice.

Exercises

1. Imagine your company makes shampoo and you want to establish yourself as a thought leader in sustainability. List five things you can measure that are connected to your product. Once you are done, go to the P&G or the Unilever website and see how they do it.
2. Look up how much electricity a factory near you uses in a year. Then measure how many homes that factory can power instead in your country. Or in another country far away.
3. Look at this sales trend. How can you write about 2019 without using all the numbers?
   2014—$3.2 million
   2015—$4 million
   2016—$7 million
   2017—$11.8 million
   2018—$21.4 million
   2019—$24.6 million

4. The sales numbers are for Tesla. What other numbers can you compare Tesla sales with to give a story context?

5. Go to a factory in your company, a restaurant down the street or a local museum. Make a list of ten things you could measure that might lead to compelling stories. Then, to gather context, add to each item something you can use to compare that measurement to something outside of your location.

6

Death by Jargon

—Fancy Words Don't Impress, They Alienate—

Overview

Get a bunch of computer programmers together and they start speaking a special language, using a specialized vocabulary only they understand. That happens with organizations too. The people inside create their own words or acronyms that become very clear to them but may be gibberish to the world outside. This is called jargon.

Your goal as a communicator is to make sure your message isn't destroyed by the use of organizational or professional jargon. As we've said, your messages should be clear and easily understood, and hopefully you've learnt some tips on how to create them that way in previous chapters. You want readers to grasp what you are saying without darting for a dictionary or re-reading what you have written.

This chapter will help you be on guard to stop jargon from creeping into your communication. The chapter will also explore common examples of company and industry jargon and help you see how to avoid it—or, at least, explain terminology, if and when you must use it.

The Jargon Trap

Why do people resort to jargon that others can't understand? The trouble is, many communicators don't just want to inform—they also want to impress. That desire to impress means many writers using big, fancy words that sound important but don't mean much. This use-to-impress and tough-to-understand language is called jargon.

That said, jargon also includes language that is specific to an industry. Sometimes, it's impossible to avoid using it. Its usage can be justified when talking to an audience that understands those terms and uses it as a language in which they communicate with one another.

For example, it would be perfectly acceptable, and even expected, of a lawyer to tell a judge that the client intends to 'execute the contents of the will'. However, when the same lawyer is talking to a client, it is more useful to tell the client to 'do as written in the will'.

The difference here is that what is perfectly clear to one type of audience could mean nothing to another. The minute you confuse your audience, you risk losing them. So while you may not be able to avoid jargon altogether, you must use it wisely.

Herd Instinct

Jargon starts off like fast fashion in clothing. We use it because leaders or trendsetters at our companies use it. Then it stays and becomes part of the company's communication style.

Writers who use jargon may not even be sure of what they are trying to say. Or they may have borrowed big words because they assume that's what people want to hear. Or because they think it adds heft to what they are saying.

More often than not, especially in corporate communication, it can be used to hide bad news or information you are unsure of. Whatever the reason, jargon is a sure way to confuse your audience and kill your message. The use of jargon is a sign of weakness in your communication style, not a strength.

Speak to Me

As we described in the first chapter, you need to speak to your audience, and in a language they can understand.

There are some ways in which we can avoid jargon. One way is to test the readability of a document. A good rule of thumb is to make sure a young teenager can understand what you are saying, just as much as your grandparent can.

If you are writing for a large audience, write for a reader who may have only basic knowledge of the subject. You should also assume that the language you write in may not even be their first language. This leaves you no choice but to use simple words.

Several governments have rules about readability of documents, especially when they involve manuals or instructions for the public. Having these rules ensures that the document is clear to the audience it is meant for and uses terms they are familiar with.

The US military, for example, uses the Flesch-Kincaid readability score for their manuals. A high score means the writing can be understood by children as young as twelve years old. Many business writers put their writing through similar readability tests to make sure it is easily understood.

But readability scores are not easy to achieve. It takes years of writing to simplify terms and write in a way that lay readers can understand. Everyone struggles with this—experts, techies and academics—because they tend to talk in the language that is understood by their peers.

As a storyteller, you have to explain for the audience, not yourself.

Business as Usual, Really?

Jargon creep is as old as management books and business-school theories, both of which have spawned a gamut of words that are now widely used by organizations. We call this corporate jargon.

Instead of telling workers they are being laid off because their jobs are gone, companies will often say they are 'right-sizing', which has resulted in redundancies. What does right-sizing really mean? The right size for a company is the wrong size for a worker who loses his/her job.

Press releases are notorious for the excessive use of the word 'synergy'. The Cambridge dictionary defines 'synergy' as 'the combined power of a group of things when they are working together that is greater than the total power achieved by each working separately'.

Take a look at this press release on the merger of two South American airlines.

LAN and TAM Announce New *Synergy Estimate* for LATAM Airlines Group
January 12, 2012 06:44 PM Eastern Standard Time

SANTIAGO, Chile--(BUSINESS WIRE)--LAN Airlines S.A. ('LAN') and TAM S.A. ('TAM') today announced a revised estimate of the *synergies* expected to be achieved through the merger of the two airlines to create LATAM Airlines Group S.A.

('LATAM Group'). LAN and TAM estimate that the combined *synergies* arising from the proposed combination could increase LATAM Group's annual operating income over time by between US$600 million and US$700 million, before depreciation and taxes, beginning four years after completion of the transaction. This represents a 50 per cent to 75 per cent increase over the initial *synergy* estimate of US$400 million per year, which the companies announced in August 2010.

The entire paragraph can be condensed to:

The combination of the two airlines is expected to boost operating income by up to 75 per cent in four years, compared to previously announced estimates.

It can be said without using the word 'synergy' at all!

The key to clear writing is: Don't make readers sweat and don't use jargon to increase word count. Readers who get bogged down by the jargon switch off. The audience gives up because you are making them work too hard to understand what you are saying. Follow the seven-second rule—if they don't get it in seven seconds, they will switch off and click away. And you have lost them.

Writers often use words bandied about by financial experts assuming it's a good way to make a big impression when talking to management. For example, when businesses say they have some 'skin in the game', all they mean is that they take some risks. The term is so widely used for risk that it's the title of a book by Nassim Nicholas Taleb. Not everyone is Taleb. And Taleb doesn't write for the lay reader.

Throwing smart-sounding words at a general audience is dumb—it's the easiest way to get them to run for cover. Never write to intimidate the reader.

Consultant Jargon

Low-hanging fruit, synergy, right-sizing, cutting-edge, brain drain, competitive advantage, deep-dive, drill down, granular, human capital, ideation, mission critical, on the same page, value add, optics, directionalize, circle back, bandwidth, ecosystem, knowledge transfer, human capital and ballpark.

A common joke about consultants is that they are people you pay to tell you what you already know. Consultants are notorious for using words that mean everything and nothing at the same time.

In 2014, a Forbes article titled 'How to Speak McKinsey' talked about the phrases widely used at the consulting firm. The author, a former McKinsey consultant called it 'fifteen quintessentially McKinsey expressions'.[*]

---

[*] Brett Arends, 'How To Speak McKinsey: 15 Key Phrases To Pass Yourself Off As A Top Management Consultant', *Forbes*, 8 January 2014, https://www.forbes.com/sites/brettarends/2014/06/08/

Let's weave some of the 'jargon' into a sentence: 'The project was low-hanging fruit, which is a really quick win that is directionally correct and was made without boiling the ocean or peeling the onion to get to version 2.0, so you see the delta.'

For those of you who are wondering, like we did, 'delta' means 'change'. The rest you must guess, for a bit of fun.

Another often-used word by consultancies everywhere is 'ecosystem'. What does it really mean? Is it a set of parameters? Is it the parts of a whole or just the overall environment?

Here is a press release that is in love with the word 'ecosystem':

OYO's Ritesh Agarwal Checks in to Bharat's Early-Stage Start-up Ecosystem with Venture Catalysts
August 18, 2020 04:22 AM Eastern Daylight Time

MUMBAI, India--(BUSINESS WIRE)--Aimed at supporting India's growing startup *ecosystem*, Ritesh Agarwal will step in as an advisor and work closely with the country's largest incubator, Venture Catalysts, to promote entrepreneurship across tier 1, 2 and 3 cities. India is a growing start-up *ecosystem* and needs experienced people to come forward

how-to-speak-mckinsey-15-key-phrases-to-pass-yourself-off-as-a-top-management-consultant/?sh=194d3aa66896 to collectively grow the *ecosystem* and make the country 'atma nirbhar bharat' (self reliant India).

All this paragraph is saying is: 'Ritesh Agarwal will be an advisor at India's largest incubator, Venture Catalyst, to encourage entrepreneurship and start-ups.'

Apply the seven-second rule and see the difference for yourself.

The overuse of jargon can kill your communication and become a habit that is hard to break out of. Be careful when you are tempted to use terms such as 'ecosystem', 'knowledge transfer', 'human capital', 'bandwidth', 'ballpark' and 'mission-critical'.

It's easier to replace 'knowledge transfer' with 'teaching', 'human capital' with 'workforce' and 'bandwidth' with 'time'. Remember you will not be 'crushing it' by using jargon, only crushing your copy.

Cultural Jargon

As a communications expert, the other minefield to avoid is cultural jargon. What's acceptable usage in one country could mean something entirely different in another.

This can sometimes even extend to simple everyday terms. If you walk into a UK store and ask for pants, you will be handed underwear, whereas in the US, you would be shown trousers.

Using jargon can get tricky. To 'table an item' in the UK means to add it to the agenda, but in the US, it means taking it off the agenda. In Asia, they could easily say 'bench an item', which means to remove it—a phrase borrowed from the software-industry practice of benching people, meaning letting them sit idle.

Cultural jargon could also be usage that is specific to one country and means little in another. A classic word is 'jugaad', which has now found its way into the Oxford dictionary. It's a Hindi word used widely in India to mean 'a flexible approach to problem-solving that uses limited resources in an innovative way'.

While readers in India will likely understand the word, chances are even neighbouring South Asians will have to reach for the dictionary to find out what it means.

As a communicator, you need to use words that are widely understood and universally accepted, regardless of where your audience is based. This is especially critical for storytelling that is going to be used in multiple countries.

Electrolux ran a successful campaign in the UK for its vacuum cleaners with the slogan 'Nothing sucks like an Electrolux'. It is not a campaign line that would have worked in the US because of the meaning of 'sucks' in American slang.

Research cultural nuances thoroughly before you dig into helping out with international and online campaigns that may be used in multiple geographies.

The Cliché Trap

The most boring way to write is to borrow an overused cliché. As a storyteller, your job is to engage readers and communicate with enthusiasm, not kill your story by peppering it with tired expressions.

Besides, some clichés have a specific context that may be well understood in one country but not in another.

'Drinking the Kool-Aid' is a cliché for believing in an idea that is doomed. The origin of the term is a 1980s' tragedy, in which some 900 members of the Peoples Temple movement died in Guyana after drinking a Kool-Aid-type drink mixed with cyanide on the order of their leader, to protest the killing of a US Congressman.

For those with no knowledge of the incident, the term makes no sense, even when used to describe an idea that is crazy.

Another commonly used and abused line is 'thinking out of the box'. Imagine this—does one think out of the box? Is the brain really a box? Not really. It's a fancy way of saying to think differently.

Is Jargon Ever Okay?

Jargon specific to an industry must be left to that closed circle of peers who use it to talk among themselves. Your job is to take those terms and simplify them without sacrificing the meaning. This means you will have to spend time becoming familiar with the industry language and then find ways to demystify it.

Several sectors are notorious for industry jargon— legal, medical, retail, technology and automobile are only some of the industries with specific terms that only insiders understand.

As a storyteller, if you stay in the industry long enough, it is easy to lose perspective on terms that are alien to outsiders. And before you know it, you will be using these words all the time, even when you're trying to communicate to generalists, rather than specialists.

Here is a classic from a press release from German carmaker BMW for an event in India:

> In contrast to other manufacturers, who use all-wheel drive principally to make up for the shortfall in traction suffered by front-wheel-drive vehicles, BMW tunes its xDrive system to provide handling typical of rear-wheel drive. Even in normal situations on the road, all-wheel-drive BMW models send the lion's share of drive to the rear wheels.[*]

To an outsider, all cars run on all wheels. Is BMW trying to say the all-wheel drive feels like a rear-wheel

---

[*] 'BMW India Showcases BMW xDrive, intelligent all-wheel drive system at the BMW Xperience 2011', *Business Wire India*, 17 October 2011, https://www.businesswireindia.com/bmw-india-showcases-bmw-xdrive-intelligent-all-wheel-drive-system-at-the-bmw-xperience-2011-28617.html

drive, which improves acceleration? Only auto-industry experts know how that works.

As an exercise, count the references to different types of wheel drives and ask yourself if a non-auto-industry expert will understand what's written. If the answer is a no, it's weak writing.

On the other hand, if this were a statement issued to a car salesperson, who knows about different types of wheel drives and can use it as a selling point to customers, it may pass.

Similarly, electric-car makers often use the term 'range anxiety' to talk about customer concern on how far the car can run on a single charge. So while the management may talk about how engineers have 'overcome range anxiety on the four wheels' by calibrating parts, as a storyteller, it's not something you can repeat to a general audience.

Now read this sentence out to a five-year-old and your oldest aunt to ask them if they can understand it: 'This four-wheel-drive guarantees you needn't have any range anxiety.' Chances are they will ask you what you meant.

You could, instead, say, 'This car runs 200 kilometres on just a single charge.'

The finance industry is also riddled with jargon. A common term is 'sweat equity', which really means that you get a stake in the business, instead of getting a fee for your work. Or doing 'due diligence of the books', which means auditing the accounts to discover the company is bang for buck, or simply put, worth the value estimated for it.

If your audience doesn't understand what you are telling them, even the most elaborate communication will get a grand burial. And that's a lot of dollars wasted.

When you do find yourself trapped in a cliché or jargon, mark out the word or the phrase. Use a dictionary and a thesaurus to find out how you can replace jargon with a simpler word or phrase. Then ask yourself if what you have rewritten is open to misinterpretation. Is it clear to someone who knows nothing about the topic?

If you do this often, you will likely catch yourself before littering your copy with jargon. It is really that easy.

Exercises

1. Rewrite the following sentences by stripping them of all jargon, so a lay reader can understand it.
    a. The deal is expected to generate approximately $900 million of run-rate cost savings and at least $500 million of revenue synergies, leading to enhanced revenue growth from expanded capabilities.
    b. The combination is expected to generate approximately $900 million of run-rate cost synergy savings over five years, driven

primarily by the elimination of duplicative corporate structures, streamlined technology infrastructure, increased operational efficiencies, process improvements and footprint optimization.

2. Match the jargon to what it means:[*]

Slippage	product
Deck	encourage
Deliverable	delay
Hard Stop	skill
Rock Star	outperformer
Core competency	deadline
Incentivize	PowerPoint presentation
Onboarding	come back
Circle back	training new employees

3. Rewrite these clichés in simple language: a foregone conclusion, a dead ringer, a no-brainer, a sweet deal, a white elephant, above board, batten down the hatches, brain drain, buy into, business as usual

4. Simplify this paragraph into a seven-second read: *With the Indian digital opportunity accelerating, many more sectors in the B2B and B2C categories*

---

[*] Liz Ryan, 'Do You Speak Corporate? Business Jargon For Humans', *Forbes*, 1 March 2016, https://www.forbes.com/sites/lizryan/2016/03/01/do-you-speak-corporate-business-jargon-for-humans/?sh=abc4f6c679ce

are emerging where technology is enabling new businesses and models. Start-ups need more broad-based operational engagement. Over the last few years, Lightspeed has expanded Lightspeed India Advisors partnership to six partners, based out of Delhi and Bengaluru.

5. Replace the following commonly used legal terms with simple words or phrases:
- Bona fide
- De facto
- Ex post facto
- Quid pro quo

7

It's All about the People

—People Love to Talk about People—

Overview

We love to hear stories about other people, especially their experiences. 'People stories' help us virtually explore new adventures. They also allow us to connect to an event or an idea by identifying with it through past personal experiences.

Companies can connect with a target audience through telling stories about their people, or their impact on people. Luckily, people stories are easy to find. If you lift the lid off any company, you'll find it is nothing without people—employees, leaders, customers. Without them, there can be no organization.

This chapter will talk about how to create stories that are human because they focus on people. It will offer tips and techniques for successful interviews. It will also address how to create stories about companies impacting people in society through corporate social responsibility (CSR) activities that build brand and customer loyalty.

The Human Connection

People want to hear stories about people. Their struggles, their triumphs, hopes and dreams, gaffes and successes. Stories about people are much more engaging than stories that focus on the product. To be appealing to existing and prospective customers and employees, a company needs to be seen as a group of people, not an abstract construction or a cold institution.

People also increasingly seek to buy from and work for companies that show compassion, empathy and a commitment to issues that matter to us. That makes it even more important to keep your company's mission meaningful in all communications. It's also an incentive to do good as a company in CSR. More about that later.

Research by consulting firm McKinsey shows that Generation Z, born between 1995 and 2010, makes purchases to express their individual identity and makes decisions based on the ethics a brand represents.[*]

---

[*] Tracy Francis and Fernanda Hoefel, '"True Gen": Generation Z and its implications for companies', McKinsey & Company, 12 November 2018, https://www.mckinsey.com/industries/

That means they want to see brands that are inclusive, whose corporate actions range from addressing global warming to eradicating bias, poverty and hunger.

People Love People Stories

Stories are what make humans human, and creating abstract worlds and concepts is what promotes human connection and cooperation, writes Yuval Noah Harari in the bestselling *Sapiens: A Brief History of Humankind*.[*] Stories create connections, empathy and trust between people.

This isn't just social science, it's neuroscience. Researchers at Princeton University mapped brain activity while a speaker was telling a real-life story.[†] The listeners' brain activity mirrored that of the speaker, meaning their brains virtually connected. Biologically, this kind of connection can prompt a wave of oxytocin, sometimes referred to as the 'bonding' hormone.

Of course, that is what we'd like to achieve in corporate communication—create connections, empathy

---

consumer-packaged-goods/our-insights/true-gen-generation-z-and-its-implications-for-companies#

[*] Yuval Noah Harari, *Sapiens: A Brief History of Humankind*, Penguin Random House India, 2015.

[†] Greg J. Stephens, Lauren J. Silbert and Uri Hasson, 'Speaker–listener neural coupling underlies successful communication', *Proceedings of the National Academy of Sciences of the United States of America*, August 2010, https://www.ncbi.nlm.nih.gov/pmc/articles/PMC2922522/

and trust, and bond with our audiences—whether they are customers, clients, prospects, employees, partners or investors.

How can you tell people stories when you're talking about a company or a product? From the 'About' section of the website, which tells the story of your company's founding, to Instagram photos of people enjoying or consuming your product or service—every piece of communication should include the people aspect, and preferably focus on the people that make your company, product or service possible and wonderful.

The next part of this chapter will tell you how to do this. Start by looking around you. Who's the founder of your organization? What influenced them to start the business? Who are the unsung heroes of your company? A barista with a keen sense of what a customer might like? A luggage handler who finds a better way to schedule shifts? A software developer with a great idea for a new function? A board member who goes above and beyond raising money for your non-profit? People are all around you, and so are stories.

How to Spotlight People

When you're ready to shine the spotlight on people in your organization, think about how you will get your information ('the story') and how you'll present it.

Before you decide, think about who your audience is. What stories do they want to hear? People want to hear about themselves and their colleagues. Second, they want to hear about change, especially change that affects them. Third, they want to hear inspiring stories about other people—to benchmark themselves and to be inspired. Read more about understanding your audience in Chapter 1, 'Message in a Bottle'.

Your storytelling should include action and emotion, preferably told as anecdotes. But how do you capture this action or emotion? The answer lies in asking questions.

The Art of the Interview

Asking great questions to garner interesting information is part science and part art. The science part is all about research and being prepared. Try to get as much information as you can about the person before you meet them. Here are some tips and tricks:

- Google them. Look for pictures and videos as well as websites with profiles of them or articles on them.
- Ask people who know them about who they are.
- Look at their LinkedIn profile and review their content, activity and comments.
- Search for them on other social media, such as Twitter and Instagram.

Once you have researched and learnt more about your subject, you are ready to prepare your interview questions. Here, it is important to ask questions that will yield answers. If you ask a yes-or-no question, the answer will be yes or no. That will stop the conversation in its tracks. Consider these tips for asking questions:

- Ask for examples.
- Use short follow-up questions, such as, 'How so?'
- Avoid double-barrelled questions (they will choose to answer the easy one only).
- Ask about their relationships. Who gives them the best advice?
- Ask about change in their lives. What happened to make them decide to change careers? Or quit their job? Or start a company?
- Ask about memories. What was their first day on the job like? How did they come up with the idea for this product?
- Ask about their experiences. What was their first job and what did they learn from it?

Asking questions to each other has been a hobby of human beings for generations. Back before the Internet and smartphones and televisions—well, all the way back to the 1800s—people created games to entertain themselves in social settings, and one famous and popular one was about asking questions. The Proust Questionnaire, as it is known, was created by

French novelist Marcel Proust. The answers are called Confession Albums and there are records of Proust answering his own questions from the 1880s. Famous people who have answered the set of questions include Karl Marx, Oscar Wilde and Paul Cézanne. The late singer David Bowie famously answered some Proust questions, stating that his greatest regret was never wearing bell-bottoms and that the quality he likes most in women is the ability to burp on command.

Proust believed the questions and answers revealed a person's true nature, and the 'game' has proved to have staying power. Today, if you look at the archives of the *Vanity Fair* magazine, you will find contemporary celebrities, from Cyndi Lauper and Melinda Gates to Pedro Almodóvar, answering some of the questions. *Vanity Fair* has an interactive website where you can answer them yourself. Other publications use these types of questionnaires as well, including *The Guardian*, especially in weekend editions.

Here are some of the Proust, and Proust-inspired, questions that might be suitable for your interviews:[*]

- What do you appreciate most in friends?
- What is your greatest fault?
- What is your idea of happiness?

---

[*] 'The Proust Questionnaire', *Vanity Fair*, August 2011, https://www.vanityfair.com/magazine/2000/01/proust-questionnaire; 'Proust Questionnaire', Wikipedia, https://en.wikipedia.org/wiki/Proust_Questionnaire

- What is your idea of misery?
- If not yourself, who would you be?
- What is your greatest fear?
- What do you consider the most overrated virtue?
- What words do you most overuse?
- Which talent would you most like to have?
- What is your greatest achievement?
- What is your most treasured possession?
- What is your greatest regret?
- What is your motto?
- What is your greatest extravagance?

Practise asking questions wherever you go, and pay attention to activities on social media that involve questions that promote engagement. Instagram has a question feature. Twitter, Facebook and LinkedIn all have tools to create polls, where you can see the results. Watch what works and adapt it to your needs.

One more thing about interviews. Be sure to audio-record them and take notes. You'll need this for quotes when you sit down to craft the story.

Connecting in the Community

We talked about how people like to read about themselves and change, and about how they increasingly care about the ethics behind a brand, a product or a company. One of the best types of stories is one where people are the cause of the change, and it is a change for the better. When disaster strikes and employees rush to help, or when they go out into the community to help improve it, they create an event worth talking about. This is storytelling about CSR. It can be company-driven or employee-driven, or both. It's especially valuable to companies because it boosts image and brand while spreading good feelings inside and outside of the company.

What Is CSR and Why Is It a Thing?

Corporate social responsibility is a broad term that addresses corporations acting more like citizens by taking part in improving society.

CSR is at the sweet spot of all the audiences a company seeks to engage. Employees want to work for a company that does philanthropic work in the community. Customers want to support brands that have empathy, get involved and contribute to positive change. Having employees act on behalf of CSR in a community of potential customers feeds all audiences.

IKEA is considered a pioneer in its CSR efforts, in social and environmental responsibility. It started producing CSR reports in 2003 and is known for its partnerships with UNICEF and Save the Children, as well as its efforts to increasingly use renewable, recycled or recyclable materials. It ranks at 97 per cent in the CSR Hub survey of 17,548 companies.[*]

---

[*] 'IKEA Group CSR/ESG Ranking', CSR Hub, https://www.csrhub.com/CSR_and_sustainability_information/IKEA-Group

CSR work in sustainability has become extremely popular as millennials and Generation Z increasingly seek to identify with companies that don't harm the earth, be it through plastic waste or contributing to global warming. Teenage climate activist Greta Thunberg personifies this growing sentiment among this demographic.

Making Sure the CSR Fits the Story

A good CSR will fit your company's mission and strategy. It's up to you as a storyteller to make sure the world is aware. Scania, the European truck maker, may choose to support safer motorways, allowing the communications team to find stories that relate to safety, where Scania can insert itself through action that can turn into a story. Miele might choose to support a cooking school, because it makes kitchen appliances. Even better, it could encourage students and graduates to teach children better cooking skills or feed the hungry.

Such CSR activities are a great source of people stories that can showcase your company's commitment to the community and its empathetic practices, and generate trust and create connections with key audiences.

Location is also important for considering where to target an audience for your storytelling. A Singapore-based company would probably want to help causes in Asia, while a German company will look in Europe—

unless it has employees or customers in another region. Wherever the company is engaged in CSR, the communications team needs to connect with the media in the local communities. This will ensure that the company actions are seen locally.

Bankers Making Change

Global bank ING sought out employees who had chosen to make changes to live more sustainably, and told their stories as a way to inspire others. The preface to the series said: 'The world has a unique chance to build back better after the coronavirus pandemic. But what about us average people? Do these unique circumstances give us some unique inspiration to make a few changes of our own?'*

The stories included the following: Marnix van der Velden, customer journey expert at ING in the Netherlands, insulated his farmhouse and installed solar panels; Fiona McDermott, an analyst at ING in New York, chose to go vegan due to the detrimental effects of animal agriculture on the environment; and Peter Kover from ING Slovakia committed to compost, reuse and recycle at home. This series highlighted employees' own initiatives rather than corporate

---

* 'Greener home, greener world', ING, 20 August 2020, https://www.ing.com/Newsroom/News/Greener-home-greener-world.htm

projects, but the initiatives coincided with ING's commitment to sustainability in its own business.

Occasions That Are Great for People Stories

CSR isn't the only way to tell stories about people, nor is it the only reason to do so. Every story about your organization should have something to say about one of your leaders, people or teams.

People like to hear about change. Here are a few typical change-driven events that happen in companies that people want to hear about.

- Career changes, starts and beginnings
- Organizational changes
- Awards
- Recognition
- Competitions
- Nominations

That's just the beginning of all the stories you can tell about how your company does what it does, in a way that will really connect. With people.

Exercises

1. Pretend you're someone else writing a feature about yourself. Write three different leads that would help people understand who you are.

2. Write ten questions for your CEO or organization leader that would interest their team.

3. List three charities or humanitarian efforts that your organization has helped in the past year. How could you tell that story? Who would be interested in it (who is your audience)? Which channels could you use to broadcast that story?

4. List three more efforts your organization could support, but isn't currently supporting. Explain why supporting them would engage employees and create a good story to tell.

5. Read a profile in the *New Yorker*, *Wired*, *The Atlantic* or *Rolling Stone* (or a similar popular magazine in your region) and write down what questions you think the writer asked to get the information that is in the story.

6. Look at the websites of companies that compete with yours, or companies that you buy products from. Find an example of a well-placed story about people. Find a place that could benefit from adding a people anecdote or story. Explain why.

PART 2

Storytelling Channels

8

Know Your Media

—Having a Meaningful Media Relationship—

Overview

Congratulations. You've finished the first section of this book covering the building blocks of story creation from message and audience to story structure and elements. Now let's turn to the channels of your communication.

In this chapter, you will learn about how media can help distribute your message, how established media organizations work across multiple mediums—from print and digital to TV and radio—and who the key media contact people may be for you. You will learn how to get their attention and how to help steer how they tell your story.

This chapter will help you take your message a step further with a better understanding of how reporters work, how newsrooms are organized and what makes it more likely they will write about you. This is traditionally called public relations or media relations.

The media and the press are just one channel for getting your story out. The following chapters in this section will look at social media, paid content, editorials and special channels that rely on audio, such as podcasting.

What Is Media Good For?

The fast-paced world of digital information and the Internet has made it easier for a company to talk directly to its target audience. It used to be that the only way to reach that audience was through a news article or an advertisement. Online reader comments on stories and social media didn't arrive until around 2000. The only way to comment was to write a letter to the editor and hope it got published.

The Internet/digital revolution ramped up change for the media and communication industries at lightning speed. Suddenly we could all see each other's letters to the editor and comments in real time. In fact, most of us skip the letter and, instead, comment freely whenever possible. Speed and transparency together are powerful in communications.

However, when everyone became able to talk directly digitally, it got loud fast. Ironically, all that noise also made it harder to get a message across. As we mentioned in the introduction to this book, with 1.7 billion websites in existence today and more than 300 billion emails being sent every day,* there's no guarantee that a well-crafted, targeted message will actually hit its mark.

In this environment, you should secure all the help you can get in order to reach your audience. The media and its reporters can offer just the boost you need in this sea of information by shining a spotlight on you.

Try to think holistically across the multiple channels addressed in this book. Depending on your target audience, your message will need to hit a number of platforms. Established media is just one of these channels. A good story in a newspaper, be it in print or digital, with a following can be your accelerator and megaphone.

Members of the media, such as reporters, photographers and editors, are useful because they have a following. They have a network of people who loyally turn to them for information. Some might argue that the media is less useful today because we can speak directly to the readers on so many other channels. However, it can be countered that the

---

* Source: The Radicati Group, Inc., https://www.radicati.com/?p=10653

media is more useful today because it offers a way to connect with the readers directly through comments, in addition to messaging from inside the stories. They help facilitate conversation and carry credibility. Using traditional media smartly can help you grow your presence.

But who are these reporters? Who is the media? Let's start with an overview of the media landscape and how reporters think when they write stories.

First, we'll look at the big picture of the media landscape. A *macro view* on the media, so to speak. Secondly, we'll delve into understanding how the reporters and editors work in a newsroom. Let's call that the *micro view* on the media. Finally, you'll need to understand the tools and elements needed for the media to communicate with its audience.

Together, with an understanding of all three parts and time spent following up with connections directly with the readers, you will be able to use the media to your benefit—to spread your message.

Media Landscape (Macro Level)

Media channels or platforms

The media can be classified by how it is delivered. There is television, radio, newspaper (print and digital), magazine (print and digital), podcasts, blogs and social media. We'll get into many of these in more detail in other chapters. Here, we'll focus on how established media feeds all these channels.

Some companies deliver their news in all formats. Bloomberg is one such company, providing news using several medium available. Some only do radio, digital and podcasts, such as NPR. Others do only TV, with short articles on the Internet, such as Sweden's national TV agency Sveriges Television. And there are digital-only news providers in India such as The Wire or The Print.

Most have gone beyond their original single medium to provide news on multiple platforms. National Geographic, for example, used to be 'just' a magazine but these days it is just as well known for its cable channel and its photos on Instagram.

Knowing all of the delivery methods of a media organization you are talking to is important because it dictates the types of content you'll want to share with them. A radio station is more likely to cover your story if you provide audio clips or access to people who can be interviewed.

Once you know your target audience, pay attention to the media they read, watch or listen to, and what format they prefer. That will help you select the media you want to interact with.

Millennials and Generation Z consumers get news online and through social media, broadly speaking. Older generations get it in print or on television. By having video ready to share, for example, you can target both.

Creators, Aggregators, Local and Social

Be aware that some media are creators of content and some are aggregators. The Associated Press (AP) is the mother of all news creators. Founded in 1846, it is a non-profit owned by news agencies. Located in more than 100 countries and serving more than a thousand newspapers, coverage by the AP feeds the English-speaking media world. Agence France-Presse (AFP) is a similar organization for the French-speaking world. They are content creators.

At the other end of the scale, there are aggregators, such as Apple News, Google News, SmartNews and Flipboard. They gather and sort news. They don't create content, but highlight it, sort it and amplify it. So, making them aware of your story may be useful once it is out there where they can select it.

There are many types of in-betweens. A local newspaper, for example, may not have a big staff, meaning it will take national news from AP but write local news in-house. If your story is local, seek out your local paper before you call AP. They are often easier to approach and eager to cover things with a local angle. Once published, you can work to spread it further via digital outlets.

All media have a presence as well on social platforms. Therefore, getting into *The New York Times* means getting printed in their newspaper as well as broadcasted on their social media feeds, again hitting multiple generations.

Media, Sorted by Region and Topic

Geography

Media can be further sliced by region. Some media are considered international, meaning they cover everything in the world. These tend to be big established national agencies, such as the AP, the AFP, Reuters and the BBC. Some agencies have regional desks in multiple locations. Reuters, for example, has more than 3,000 reporters in 200 countries.

Then there are national publications that target readers in their own countries, such as *USA Today*, *Le Monde*, Telemundo, *China Daily* and the *Times of India*. These publications cover everything that happens inside the country and anything outside that relates back to the country. They also cover significant international news.

Topics

Geography aside, there are news platforms that only focus on specific interests. These include lifestyle interests from guns to cooking; political interests from conservative to liberal; and academic interests from history to psychology. The list is long.

The larger news outlets will have reporters for multiple topics. So, a reporter at *The New York Times* may work for a New York-based paper but only cover culture and arts in Europe. If you have a story about clean energy in India, they are probably not the right reporter for you.

Still, it's good to think broadly about all topics. If you can find a link between your company and a specific news area that people are interested in, you won't want to miss that opportunity. That clean energy story might just be of interest to a political reporter about to cover a climate-change summit.

Think about how your organization might be related to popular topics. What are some of the most popular things people want news about? They include breaking news, politics, crime, sports and the weather. So, if your company sells umbrellas, you want to connect with the weather reporter as well as the fashion reporter. Or, if you sell an app to find lost cell phones, you want to be connected to the consumer reporter, the technology reporter and the crime reporter.

For each of the news topics above, there are dozens, if not hundreds, of online news sites, magazines and shows. Food and cooking alone is a long category list. Take a moment to look at a news app such as Flipboard and see the list of magazines and sources in each topic area.

When it comes to what's most popular on YouTube video games come first, followed by politics/current events and sports. At BBC, sports is the most popular type of news.

The bottom line is that you need to figure out which topics align with your message in different locations and mediums. If your company makes trucks, you potentially want to be commenting on transportation, community development, business development, road safety, weather and more.

Types of Media Ownership

Media ownership is increasingly consolidated. By 2017, for example, 90 per cent of the media in the US was owned by just five companies.* Just forty years ago, fifty companies shared control of that same percentage. Around the world, non-state-owned media is dominated by family-owned businesses. Silvio Berlusconi in Italy; Alex Springer AG and Bertelsmann AG in Germany; and Rupert Murdoch in the US and the UK.

Ownership may lead to bias in the coverage the media outlet offers you. A newspaper that is owned by a politician, an industry leader or a friend of a politician or an industry leader may have an opinion about your company and its products that will colour their coverage.

In many countries, there is also state-run media. In the US, NPR is funded by the state and its listeners. In the UK, the state funds the BBC. Some countries have fairly free and fair coverage. The BBC, AFP and NPR

---

* Source: Wikipedia, https://en.wikipedia.org/wiki/Concentration_of_media_ownership

are often mentioned as examples. In other countries, there may be less freedom.

Knowing how much control a state has over its news agencies, or who a private owner is, may impact how you interact with it. This varies greatly by country, so if you are looking for coverage in a new country, spend some time understanding the ownership landscape.

In India, the public service broadcaster is called Prasar Bharti, which operates the All India Radio and Doordarshan, the national television channel.

That said, the hyper-competitive news environment in India is dominated by private media companies. One of the largest news conglomerates, Bennett, Coleman & Co. Ltd, was founded in 1838. It is a family-owned business that boasts the world's most-circulated English-language newspaper, the *Times of India*, and India's most-read business paper, the *Economic Times*. It also owns television channels, regional language papers, movie channels, radio channels and websites. Three of the other large media companies are also family-run.

The political climate in general may impact bias in coverage everywhere in the world. This may be driven by the financial state of the news outlet or simply the power wielded by the government.

It is not unusual to find that news coverage may not be wholly impartial to the government or even minority shareholders of the media organizations.

Go Local

Most local communities have media that focuses on the neighbourhood. Most have gone online as a more cost-efficient way to communicate than to print and deliver papers. Local radio also thrives with a committed audience, which tunes in regularly for traffic and weather, at the very least.

Wherever your company has people, production or customers is where you should be connected with the local media outlets.

Local opinion page writers tend to be read by almost everyone in the community. In the US, radio reached more Americans than any other platform in 2019, according to Nielsen.[*]

Local talk shows reach local audiences better than national or international ones. If you can get a placement with these local mouthpieces, you're getting a laser target for your message, albeit in a limited local environment.

Newsroom Structure (Micro Level)

Types of Organizational Structures

Media organizations may be sorted by topic covered, region, time of day and medium. Often, it is a matrix

---

[*] 'The Steady Reach of Radio: Winning Consumer Attention', Nielsen.com, 17 June 2019, https://www.nielsen.com/us/en/insights/article/2019/the-steady-reach-of-radio-winning-consumers-attention/

of all. At a large organization, you may need to find the tech reporter in Hungary and the tech reporter for TV. One may be in Budapest and the other in London or New York, and they may not talk to each other.

It's important to know the region a reporter or editor is responsible for, as well as their industry or topic beat. There's no point in pitching your company's story to a reporter who writes about blue-chip start-up technology stocks when you are a medium-sized maker of dog food. Sure, she's a stock reporter and you have listed shares, but it's not the right match.

In addition to being sorted by region, a news agency can be organized by topic or by channel.

How the Media Selects News

It's essential to understand who the media people are and what they need. At the end of the day, there are some basic things all reporters need to create a story. It must be of interest to their audience and backed by facts.

We'll start by looking at how stories come to reporters. Then we'll talk about how to package these elements, which are valuable to the reporter, to facilitate the creation of news that amplifies your message.

How Reporters Work

Most newsrooms have a workflow, and this may vary from newsroom to newsroom, depending on how many mediums they are available in and how integrated the various departments are. This is typically how news coverage and assignments flow between reporters for a press release or breaking news:

Flash Desk: These are editors that sit at computers or telephones and write fast sentences for quick dissemination.

Main Desk: Once a news flash is sent, there are reporters who write quick stories and updates about the news as it is breaking. In a newspaper, the beat reporter is often called upon to fill in the breaking news.

Beat Reporters: These reporters take over when the story is big and looks like it will gather an audience. They have contacts in their specific industry or beat. These are the people you want to start talking to.

Feature Reporters: These reporters follow really big stories or trends. Their stories may have different angles than the breaking news. These stories have a longer shelf life because of their angle, analysis, interviews or links to historical events, for example. The stories live on in newspapers, podcasts, documentaries and magazines. You'll want to know this group too.

Influencers: Influencers are the exception here. They don't necessarily work in a newsroom or cover news, but if you want them to talk about your message, they will need the same elements as the reporters. Read more about them in the social media chapter. However, be aware that influencers can be on traditional radio as well as in the social channels.

There are a number of ways a news tip reaches a reporter. It can come through a press release, online or via email. It can happen at an event such as a press conference. It can be an idea they have that is pitched to an editor by a communicator such as you. It can also be an idea from an editor that is assigned to the reporter. It can be something they are chasing that a competitor has or something they see on social media or another channel.

Multiple Ways into a Newsroom

Above, you read about how a breaking news item might flow through different types of reporters and regions. They, too, get help along the way. All the people that help them can propose your message for a story if they know about you. Here are some of the other media people you may want to get to know.

Editors: Editors typically assign stories to reporters. Also, they get a final say on content before it is used. They also help suggest sources and data to fill out a story. If they know about you, they might suggest a story based on you or suggest you as an expert source to interview. There are also desk editors, whose role is to make the reporter's writing better.

Photo Editors: Photo editors are crucial for web and print publication. If you get your photos into their photo library, you boost your chances of showing up in stories that are related to your message. Photo editors are always looking to build their library.

Video Editors: The same goes for video editors. They help convert the raw footage that has been gathered by the camera crew and convert it into a story that can be used on-air. Ever wonder why when breaking news happens, the video footage behind the anchor gets repeated over and over? That's because they don't have enough relevant footage to fill it out. Offer TV stations the chance to come to your facilities to take footage or send it to them for their libraries if your footage is relevant to the news story. Read more about this in the sound and video chapter.

Opinion Editors: Most traditional media outlets have an opinion section for editorials and columnists. Editorials are usually statements made by the editorial leadership about current issues. They are the opinion of the newspaper. Columnists also write opinion articles but usually specialize in a topic, as Nobel-laureate Paul Krugman writes about the economy in *The New York Times*. Columnists are always looking for new angles. The opinion pages are also open to guest columnists, should you want to write your own opinion for publication. We'll talk more about topic positioning for leaders in Chapter 12, 'Take Me to Your Leader'.

TV and Radio Bookers: The bookers are key people in non-print newsrooms. Anchors need to be interviewing and talking to people. A booker can call up to fifty people in a day just to get enough 'yes' responses to fill a show. If you are knowledgeable about a topic that helps promote your message or shine a light on you, make sure the bookers have your number and call them when you've got something to say about breaking news.

Make Their Job Easy

To get a reporter to write about your story, you have to make their jobs easy by giving them everything they need to know in what's called a 'pitch'. You will learn in many of the other chapters how to create assets for your own messaging on your own channels, from your website to your intranet.

These same assets can be served to reporters and editors to entice them to write about you. Reporters are busy people and preparing a short, concise presentation of the story with supporting assets will help the story be memorable. This is called a pitch.

Take your message, the one you worked on in Chapter 3, 'Story Alchemy', and package it with supporting assets into your pitch. Help the reporter by offering a good angle or hook to the story. Make the hook exclusive to them. It might be something that connects directly to their local audience. The pitch might be in an email. If so, the headline practice you did in Chapter 2, 'Killer Headlines', will help you write an attention-grabbing subject line.

Make your pitch more enticing by adding back-up information and resources through links. This makes their reporting journey easier. And don't forget to include images, infographics and videos, as discussed in separate chapters. Compelling visual assets will also make their job easier. Who knows, you may get a reporter or an editor who suddenly has an open slot and needs a story. Last-minute changes happen. If your material is sitting on their desk, wrapped with a bow, you're going to be considered. Make sure your message is in the right place at the right time.

Finally, remember reporters and editors are people too. It doesn't hurt to build a relationship with them by staying in touch and showing you are interested in what they do. Consider keeping a spreadsheet of the reporters writing on topics that are relevant to your business and tracking when you talk to them, when you've shared things with them and what they've written about lately.

Here's the structure of a successful pitch:

1. Start with the lead of a possible story. A 'what' and 'why' lead or a 'what and so-what' lead. Follow the guidelines in Chapter 3, 'Story Alchemy'.

2. Include why the reporter's readers would care. What's the context or the connector for them?
3. Include relevant assets from data to images to video.
4. Be clear about your call to action. What do you want the reporter to do: write, review, interview and/or visit?
5. Offer access to interesting people in your organization.
6. Make it clear that something is exclusive to them if that is the case.
7. Make access to the exclusivity time-sensitive to add a sense of urgency.
8. Don't forget to include your contact details and make sure you are accessible.
9. Make sure your email subject line grabs their attention.

Exercises

1. List five media organizations or publications you would seek to get attention for the following messages or products. Explain why.

- A new type of dishwashing liquid.
- A new clothing-recycling charity for a company that makes washing machines.
- A restructuring of top management at a blue-chip company that makes computers.

- A new series of funding for a start-up that makes chocolate.

2. You work for a company that is going to launch a new consumer product in New Zealand. Do the following things to prepare:
- Make a list of the main media outlets, print, radio and TV.
- Consider which sections of each outlet might be interested in your company, your product and your leaders.
- Write down the names of the reporters covering past stories in these areas, along with their contact details.

3. Your company is going to build a factory in Nova Scotia, Canada. You want to establish good local relations there. Come up with three ways you can use local media to reach the local audience.

9

Communicating on Social

—Go Where the Eyeballs Are—

Overview

Social media exploded in the early 2000s. It happened so fast and on such a scale that teenagers today only know life with multiple social media connections, from Facebook to Twitter to Instagram, to name some of the more established channels.

Social media has become a major source of customers, product sale and employee engagement. In some ways, the traditional storytelling techniques apply. In others, the rules have completely changed. We'll cover that in this chapter.

Let's be clear up front—we won't address every type of social media out there. That would require a slew of books that would all be out of date as soon as they were published. Instead, we will look at some of the most popular channels out there for companies and organizations, and offer examples and tips that will apply across the board.

With the basics covered here, you'll also see us dig into some of these channels again in further chapters from leadership branding to crisis communications and corporate publications.

A New Landscape

Social media is not useful without a strategy. Anyone can create an account on Facebook or Instagram and pump out content. In fact, the challenge is that just about everyone does. Social media is crowded and loud, making it hard to rise above the din.

That said, social media has democratized talent, good ideas and products as has also created stars, hero products and lasting ideas.

In the new media world, a great singer doesn't need to chase a fancy record label to gain fame—YouTube popularity can bring the big-name record company to their doorstep. A raft of celebrities today are social media superstars who are also traditional media stars—from Canadian comedian and actor Lilly Singh to US stand-up comic Sarah Cooper, who rose to cult status mocking former US president Donald Trump on Twitter. And then you have celebrities built by traditional media, such as Paris Hilton, who has teamed up with YouTube for a documentary called *This Is Paris*, in which she claims to show her real self.

In 2017, Mashable ran a story about a university in China that offers a course on social media stardom, hoping to make its students social media stars.*

Red Bull is a classic case study in how an energy drink maker used powerful storytelling across multiple platforms to become a multimedia powerhouse. It has a YouTube channel with more than 9 million subscribers, a strong presence on Facebook, Instagram and Twitter, and does storytelling on its website.

The Red Bull example tells us that whatever the medium, the basic rules of good content apply.

How Social Are You?

Social media has changed rapidly since 2004, when everyone was excited about a social networking platform called Facebook, launched by a fresh-faced college dropout named Mark Zuckerberg, along with his roommates.

Facebook has grown into the largest social media platform in the world and spawned a culture of putting your (well-curated) life out there for everyone to see, or at least for your family and friends to see.

---

* Yvette Tan, 'Want to become a social media celeb? There's a college degree for that', Mashable, 20 June 2017, https://mashable.com/2017/06/20/wanghong-china-social-media-star/?utm_cid=hp-h-1#R1XELY6MEqqR

In the past decade, WhatsApp, Instagram, Pinterest, Twitter, WeChat, Tumblr, Snapchat, TikTok, Qzone, Telegram, Hike, Clubhouse, Twitch and many others have flooded the market, giving users choice and storytellers a headache.

Choosing the right platform, or platforms, is no longer simple. It requires pages of insight and data if you are going to spend money and chase outcomes. It's even more difficult to predict with any certainty what will go viral, which is the aim of most storytelling done by brands.

It's also important to be in the loop on how social media platforms change their algorithms and how that may affect the visibility of your posts, though good-quality content tends to get better play.

It doesn't always take a big agency or big bucks to garner attention. In 2015, a fierce debate broke out on Twitter over the colour of a dress. #TheDress was posted first on Tumblr by a user, asking if it was gold and white, or blue and black. For twenty-four hours, people in every corner of the world weighed in. Since then, several Twitter hashtags have gone viral.

The same holds for content on other social media platforms but we will talk about that in detail later.

The Right Matrix

Social media usage differs greatly by country. India is Facebook's biggest market, followed by the US, Indonesia, Brazil, Mexico and the Philippines.

Break it down by age, though, and Facebook is more popular with older generations. Young adults are more likely to be on Instagram, or TikTok while teens talk on Snapchat. Unless these are banned in their countries. In that case, they migrate to WhatsApp or other vehicles.

Beyond age and demographics, also consider the message. Facebook has a lot of text and photos, and now it does livestream, which is popular too. Twitter, of course, allows just limited characters of text but you can add images too, or do polls and post GIFs. Instagram and Pinterest are all about images and videos rather than text, and, of course, you can 'go live' on Instagram as well.

Twitter has more than 350 million global monthly users, but 262 million of them are outside the US, with Japan and India leading usage. It tends to be used for breaking news and instant opinion. India has the most Facebook users, with over 310 million, followed by the US, with 190 million. More men use Twitter. More women use Pinterest. More Americans use LinkedIn, and messaging there is focused on topics for the workplace and business. People over fifty years of age don't use Snapchat and people over forty don't usually grab TikTok to share and consume content.*

---

* Source: https://blog.hootsuite.com/twitter-statistics and https://blog.hootsuite.com/social-media-demographics/

The takeaway from this book is that before you start creating a post on one of these sites, you should consider the following to help you make sure you are choosing the best medium for your message.

- Generation/age
- Gender
- Geographical location
- Format—length of text, visual, video

To summarize, a company may choose a social media platform because of anything from location to message to audience, so setting a strategy is important.

Let's dig into some of the most popular platforms.

LinkedIn

This is the social media platform of choice for most businesses and professionals.

There are more than 720 million LinkedIn users, of which 76 per cent are outside the US. The second-biggest group of users are in India, followed by China and Brazil. More than half of the users are college graduates. It is the top channel for B2B (business-to-business) marketing. Who owns LinkedIn? Microsoft.[*]

---

[*] 'LinkedIn by the Numbers: Stats, Demographics & Fun Facts', Omnicoreagency.com, last updated on 6 January 2021, https://www.omnicoreagency.com/linkedin-statistics/

LinkedIn is adding a lot of new tools for marketing, selling and branding. But companies don't just use LinkedIn to generate business and sell. Many use it to tell their stories. In the same way, an individual can use this channel to build their personal brand, and companies can use it to build their own narrative.

The audience of LinkedIn is professional. It is people looking for employment, project work, advice on management, building a network, innovative ideas, being a better leader and being more efficient—just to name a few.

LinkedIn has a number of ways to market, such as live video, events and articles. That's also an opportunity to tell stories. This is where you will apply the skills you learnt in other chapters on writing, images and engagement.

There are a few things you must remember about LinkedIn, and it's what we call 'dress-for-office content'. LinkedIn is like turning up for work in work clothes. They can be casual—but should not include your pyjamas.

LinkedIn is the place where your peers, industry leaders and competition will watch you and your company. So the stories must link back to your professional acumen.

While it may be nice to tell your Facebook friends that you spent the weekend gardening, if you want to mention it on LinkedIn, it's better to tell your LinkedIn friends what gardening taught you about nurturing colleagues in the workplace.

The topics on LinkedIn can be on anything from female empowerment to better governance, ethics to entrepreneurship, and innovation to climate change. The stories you choose to tell there must reveal something about your brand values or company profile.

Using LinkedIn, companies can alert all employees with a notification once a day when something is posted on the corporate account. That's a direct way to externally reach what used to be considered only an 'internal' audience. It also allows employees to help you broadcast your message louder and further.

LinkedIn allows 'posts' for shorter pieces and 'articles' for longer ones. You can post them on other social media handles too. An article is typically a blog post and the more frequently you post them, the more likely it is to bring you attention.

It also allows other LinkedIn users to connect with you or just follow you. LinkedIn has its own list of influencers. Here is what LinkedIn says about this list:

> LinkedIn Influencers are selected by invitation only and comprise a global collective of 500+ of the world's foremost thinkers, leaders, and innovators. As leaders in their industries and geographies, they discuss newsy and trending topics such as the future of higher education, the workplace culture at

Amazon, the plunge in oil prices, and the missteps of policymakers.*

As a storyteller, you could either become an influencer or, if you are helping your leadership team build a profile, you could start by getting them to post powerful thought pieces that will get read and noticed.

LinkedIn publishes its annual list of influencers both by country and globally. Several women lead the list, including Christine Lagarde, president of the European Central Bank, Jacinda Ardern, the prime minister of New Zealand, and Melinda Gates, co-chair of the Bill & Melinda Gates Foundation.

YouTube

YouTube is the most used social media platform and one that is often overlooked and misunderstood by Generation X and boomers. YouTube is the second-most-used search engine after Google. There are 2 billion active monthly users on the video platform.

No matter how you look at it, YouTube ranks high. Consider age and gender demographics. Also, almost half of YouTube users are under thirty-five, and just more than 60 per cent of them are men. More than 80 per cent of fifteen- to twenty-five-year-olds use

---

* 'LinkedIn Influencers', LinkedIn.com, 4 October 2019, https://www.linkedin.com/help/linkedin/answer/49650/linkedin-influencers?lang=en

YouTube. The fastest-growing user groups are those that are over thirty-five and over fifty-five.[*]

Consider usage and demand. There are some 5 billion views of videos each day. About two-thirds of YouTube traffic comes from outside the US. A quarter of the views are on mobile devices.

A third of all Internet traffic belongs to YouTube. And content moves fast. Remember the 'Gangnam Style' video in 2013? It was so popular, it broke YouTube's counter. But users are selective. One in five users will leave if they don't like the first ten seconds of a video. And they'll tell you if they don't like it. The video of Justin Bieber's *Baby* has 11 million dislikes.[†]

But who comes to YouTube? It covers so many needs. The list is exhausting. According to Think with Google, a website that offers data and insights, the two top reasons people come to YouTube are to 'relax' and 'feel entertained'.

Here are some categories that dominate:[‡]

- Comedy: Everyone from stand-up comics to regular TV comedy shows can be found on YouTube.

[*] Karin Olafson and Tony Tran, '100+ Social Media Demographics That Matter to Marketers in 2021', Hootsuite, 27 January 2021, https://blog.hootsuite.com/social-media-demographics/

[†] 'YouTube by the Numbers: Stats, Demographics & Fun Facts', Omnicore, 2 April 2021, https://www.omnicoreagency.com/youtube-statistics/

[‡] 'The latest YouTube stats on when, where, and what people watch', Thinkwithgoogle.com, https://www.thinkwithgoogle.com/data-collections/YouTube-stats-video-consumption-trends/

Comedy is what people turn to to feel good, and there are several comedy actors who are used by companies to promote products in a humorous way. Lilly Singh has nearly 15 million subscribers. She endorses brands by melding them with her storytelling, so it doesn't feel like an obvious hard sell. Shaadi.com, the Indian matchmaking site, often uploads funny videos on romance and relationships. In 2017, it showcased stand-up comic Neeti Palta, which got more than 3.4 million views.

- Entertainment: YouTube is also the place to go to watch movies and TV. Many cable cord-cutters get their television in bite-sized clips on YouTube. Companies ranging from Hyundai to LG and Samsung have successfully used it in India to make viral short films. Actor Priyanka Chopra used YouTube to host a talk show with A-listers, called *If I Could Tell You Just One Thing*, which has millions of viewers. According to Statista.com, the most-watched entertainment channel on YouTube is the Indian music label and movie studio T-Series, with 155 million subscribers as of May 2021.[*]

- Music: The most famous YouTuber in music is Justin Bieber. Shawn Mendes also started there.

[*] H. Tankovska, 'Most Viewed YouTube Channel Owners of All Time as of May 2021, by Views', Statista.com, 3 June 2021, https://www.statista.com/statistics/373753/most-viewed-youtubers-all-time/

South Korean band BTS got more than 100 million views within the first twenty-four hours of uploading their music video 'Butter' on YouTube. Luis Fonsi and Daddy Yankee's 'Despacito' has more than 6 billion views. Need we say more?

- How-to: YouTube is the place to go to learn how to do something. From how to fix your outdoor grill to how to parallel-park a car, there's a video for everything. There are millions of videos on make-up, fashion and art. It's a great place for companies to offer tutorials on how to do things related to their products, directly or indirectly. US home-improvement chain Home Depot has a YouTube channel with how-to videos that help promote its products, from paint and tiles to gardenware. Its most popular video tells viewers how to install a toilet and has more than 3 million views; it is more than a decade old.

- Education: YouTube is also the place to go to learn things, from coding to history. There are videos on YouTube to help you learn things we used to only learn in a classroom setting. Byju's, one of the world's most valuable education technology companies, Khan Academy and Ted-Ed are among those that teach on YouTube.

For storytellers, YouTube offers a great way to get the dedicated attention of users to help push a purchase or get familiar with a brand. According to Think with Google, 68 per cent users watched YouTube to help make a purchasing decision. This is why it's an important platform for companies too.

Businesses may not always use the channel to create messages about buying—perhaps they just use it to recreate memories or spread a powerful social message that resonates with your brand. It could promote the arts and culture by sponsoring events that can be showcased on YouTube.

Coke Studio by Coca-Cola, which encourages local music talent, has a strong following in South Asia, including India and Pakistan. Some of the music performances have more than 300 million views and 2 million likes.

Several brands in India have used YouTube to tell memorable, emotional stories to connect with customers. Hyundai did a few short videos to mark twenty years in the Indian car market, which they called 'Creating 20 Years of Brilliant Moments', which got more than 200 million views.

Vogue India ran a successful series on women's empowerment called #StartWithTheBoys to campaign for gender sensitization. The storyline was 'Boys Don't Cry', to talk of how our roles are set in childhood and that leads to discrimination and violence against women in adulthood. The video got more than 2 million views on YouTube.

As with all other content, YouTube also needs you to write good descriptions that will show up in a search for the content to be found in the first place. Furthermore, the video needs to have a decent quality of sound and footage—don't underestimate this. YouTube itself is full of tutorials on how to make better YouTube videos.

Facebook

Facebook has the most users and it's been around the longest. That said, it has dipped into multiple controversies around sharing user information with third parties and allegedly colluding with vested parties in selecting and deselecting news; failure to remove hate posts; spreading fake news; streaming violence; and more.

Zuckerberg has had to spend several uncomfortable hours answering governments and public interest groups. This has prompted users to leave the platform and start campaigns such as #DeleteFacebook and #UnfriendFacebook.

As a storyteller for your company, the first thing to identify is whether being on Facebook may adversely affect your brand image because of user mistrust generated by these controversies. Celebrities such as Jim Carrey quit the platform and high-profile brands such as Elon Musk's Tesla and SpaceX deleted their pages.

Still, given that it is the largest social media platform, that's not an easy choice. Many celebrities have used Facebook to promote causes and charities, such as the ALS IceBucketChallenge, which raised $220 million worldwide to fund research on amyotrophic lateral sclerosis (ALS).

Celebrities, sportspeople and heads of state joined in with all of those who poured a bucket of ice-cold water on their heads in twenty-four hours or donated to support research towards a cure for ALS. The likes of Bill Gates, Jeff Bezos, Sheryl Sandberg and Tim Cook took part, as well as more than 28 million additional people.

One brand that has consistently used Facebook to engage audiences is Oreo, the cookie brand that belongs to Kraft Foods. You could say Oreo lives on Facebook. Their page has 41 million likes.

Oreo has campaigned for different countries, from Pakistan to the Philippines to the US. Its campaigns have included the Oreo recipe contest, an augmented-reality Oreo cookie game on Facebook, and even simple ones such as #Playwithoreo, where people shared their photos showing how they enjoyed their Oreo cookies.

Many businesses use Facebook to run advertising. It's easy to target the audience using Facebook filters by age, gender, geography, interests and so on.

The flip side of Facebook's reach is that for messaging gone wrong, the backlash can be huge.

Dove, a Unilever brand of personal care products, had to pull advertising on Facebook that showed a black woman turn white after using Dove body wash.

Dove apologized to customers, who called the ad racially insensitive.

Pepsi Sweden used a Facebook post to show a Cristiano Ronaldo voodoo doll on a train track getting smashed by a Pepsi can before the World Cup qualifier in 2013. The match was between Portugal and Sweden and the backlash was so strong that they took it down and apologized to the footballer.

As a storyteller, create content that is respectful to your audience wherever in the world they may be. The digital medium knows few geographical boundaries and a backlash can result in a decline in sales and loss of brand value globally.

WhatsApp

The messaging app owned by Facebook (which also owns Instagram, by the way) is used by companies for internal communications, making WhatsApp groups out of work teams. Some employees are reluctant to use their private phone numbers for work purposes, however, and other privacy concerns have emerged.

Nevertheless, businesses small and large are turning to WhatsApp Business to take orders and respond to customer queries. Medical, dental and veterinary offices, as well as restaurants and beauty salons, use WhatsApp to confirm appointments and reservations. Some have stepped up their WhatsApp game to offer online medical consultations, send new product offers or discounts, and use images, audio files or short video clips to stay in touch with current customers.

This can help your brand communication be interactive. In India, Colgate invited people to send selfies of their smile via WhatsApp to a phone number displayed on the toothpaste pack for a chance to win a makeover by fashionista and actor Sonam Kapoor's stylist.

You may not see big corporations in Europe and America allowing the use of WhatsApp for employees because they deem it a possible security issue. But global companies will find that employees do it anyway, on the sly.

Twitter

Some of the biggest users of Twitter include airlines, sports organizations, gaming companies and political organizations, as well as many big companies around the world.

Twitter is where polarization happens more often than not, and it is a tricky platform for that very reason.

Every second counts on Twitter. For airlines, it is the place people go to, to complain about delayed flights or other problems. Because customer service deals with its customers here in a transparent and open forum, how they respond affects the reputation of the company.

Make sure your Twitter customer representatives have had communications training and are well looped in on corporate messaging, marketing and brand image.

For sports, this is the place fans hang out and talk. When matches are in play, most fans are watching the game in person or on television, while also watching the conversation on Twitter.

UEFA Champions League uses its @ChampionsLeague handle, with more than 34 million followers, to promote the game, players and matches to engage fans and boost their reputation.

So, if you are a brand that sells a beverage that sports fans tend to drink, you also want your marketing team on Twitter targeting sporting events. Red Bull, Coca-Cola and PepsiCo do this all the time.

Athletes often post brand endorsements on Twitter and it's a great way for brands to reach a captive audience. Indian cricketer Virat Kohli has more than 42 million followers on Twitter and he routinely uses his account to post clips of brands he is endorsing or social causes he is involved in, aside from personal tweets and the game itself.

Companies do often pay-per-tweet, which is built into the endorsement contract they sign with celebrities.

Twitter has also been used successfully to upend rival brands. During the Super Bowl in 2015, Volvo ran #VolvoContest, which asked viewers to tweet the name of a person they would give a Volvo to and why, whenever they saw an automobile company commercial on TV. With a much lower spend than rivals, Volvo ended up being the most-talked-about brand during the advertisement breaks.

Companies also seek out Twitter for creating a distinct brand personality.

Charmin, a brand of toilet paper, uses Twitter to take on a cheeky or sarcastic tone in places where it would be more buttoned-up on, say, LinkedIn.

Twitter is also a great place for high-impact campaigns using creative hashtags. Charmin's campaign included #TweetFromTheSeat.

Many not-for-profits use Twitter to create awareness and raise funding by running campaigns. ALS's #IceBucketChallenge was as popular on Twitter as Facebook.

Two of the recent campaigns that got a lot of love on Twitter were #BlackLivesMatter, in the fight for racial equality, and #MeToo, in the fight for gender equality and against sexually predatory behaviour towards women. Both can be called civil campaigns, rather than corporate branding, but they are good examples of Twitter campaigns that know no geographical boundaries.

Twitter, just like Facebook, is multilingual and offers a lot of scope for hyperlocal campaigns.

Twitter will also see brands get funny with each other. In a famous interaction between Netflix India and other global brands, after Netflix tweeted #SeduceSomeoneInFourWords. Everyone from makers of condoms to pizza companies responded with lines such as 'Your place or mine?' and 'Come over. There's pizza.'

Companies often have multiple handles to talk to different audiences. This applies to Twitter and other social platforms. Amazon's handles include @amazonmusic, @amazonbooks, @amazon and @amazonhelp.

You will find a lot of content duplication from companies on LinkedIn and Twitter. More likely than not, you will see more humorous exchanges on Twitter.

Twitter: Social Listening Tool

Twitter can also be a medium for pressuring companies or individuals to act. Elon Musk, the founder of Tesla and SpaceX, deleted the Facebook accounts of his company after 'Twitterati' called for it. Yes, that's the name for those who use Twitter heavily.

Brands also use Twitter for crisis communications because of the immediacy of reach.

If you are going to be on Twitter, you have to be always on. Of all the social media channels, this is the one that makes a minute seem a lifetime, so any delay in responding on Twitter can quickly cascade into an unmanageable crisis of communication.

Twitter runs a blog that helps people use Twitter more effectively for communications.

There are many companies that use software to trawl through the millions of conversations on Twitter to analyse user preferences. Brands often use these insights to craft their messaging or tweak their storytelling to make it more appealing to users.

As a storyteller, having these insights can help you deliver more appealing content and avoid crafting low-impact messages.

Instagram

If images are your hook, Instagram is your go-to. Now owned by Facebook, more than 50 billion photos have been uploaded to Instagram so far.[*]

The top category on Instagram is fashion. That said, automakers and food companies are using it to promote their goods and services and engage with users.

Celebrities use it heavily. Footballer Cristiano Ronaldo has the most followers on Instagram, according to Statista.com.[†]

---

[*] 'Instagram by the Numbers: Stats, Demographics & Fun Facts', Omnicoreagency.com, 6 January 2021, https://www.omnicoreagency.com/instagram-statistics/

[†] H. Tankovska, 'Instagram Accounts with the Most Followers Worldwide as of February 2021 (in Millions)', Statista.com, 18 March 2021, https://www.statista.com/statistics/421169/most-followers-instagram/

Instagram uses hashtags like Twitter, and short videos like YouTube, has a 'live' function like the others and a 'story' function, in which a post is only online for twenty-four hours unless you add it to your 'highlights'. The story function was pioneered by Snapchat and copied by Instagram and later Facebook and LinkedIn.

Nike has more than 150 million followers on Instagram, and a lot of luxury goods makers, from Chanel to Louis Vuitton, are on Instagram with drool-worthy images and millions who follow them. They use it for everything from product promotions to boosting their brand values.

Instagram offers filters and add-ons to make images pop and make them more visually arresting. The image with the most likes on Instagram is an egg.

But storytelling on Instagram can go beyond just an image. Justin Bieber shared an emotional post in 2019 about his depression and drug use. Others use it to announce pregnancies, weddings and so on.

Even traditional media is taking to Instagram to promote stories and, with the launch of Instagram Shops, more and more businesses might be attracted to this medium.

Using Instagram Engagement Tools

Some companies use Instagram to feature employees at work and in society as well. Marriott, for example, uses a handle, 'Marriott Careers', to showcase employees having fun at work as a way to attract employees.

So, if it's Take Your Kid to Work Day, a company may want to put those pictures on Instagram instead of LinkedIn.

Companies are also using Instagram to reach their employees and appear appealing to future employees.

For example, the question sticker invites employees and followers to engage in a question. That's an opportunity to use followers to create content. Ask employee followers a question such as: What was the best piece of advice you got from a colleague at work? The answer can be used to make a BuzzFeed-inspired list that can be posted externally but also internally.

Equally engaging are Instagram polls, Q&As, pop quizzes and countdowns. They all do two valuable things. First, they engage people with your organization. Second, they generate content in the form of tips, best-of lists, suggestions, etc. That's on top of simply using location, people mentions and hashtags.

Instagram is also a popular place for competitions with pictures. An example is BabyBjörn, the maker of baby carriers. Its Instagram page asks people to post pictures of their 'BabyBjörns' to get featured. What is a BabyBjörn without a baby in it? And who doesn't love a cute baby picture? They're made for Instagram.

Instagram may rank #6 in active users, but it ranks #1 in another way. That's when counting followers.

Influencers are important for the promotion of everything from fashion to jobs to ideas. Additionally, the most-followed influencers are on Instagram. But what is an influencer?

Influencers

Messages can be boosted on social media through the use of influencers. These are people who have a following. It may be a news commentator on YouTube, or a celebrity such as Ariana Grande on Instagram. These people have thousands or millions of followers and can discreetly or openly promote your product for a price.

The top influencers on Instagram include Cristiano Ronaldo, Kylie Jenner, Selena Gomez, and Leo Messi. They each have more than 200 million followers. These are all big celebrities and people will try to tag them in their own posts to get attention.

On YouTube, influencers are measured also by how much money they make on their channels. In 2019, Ryan Kaji was the highest paid, at $26 million. At eight years old, he lives in Texas and has 29 million followers. He reviews new toys on his channel 'Ryan's World'.

Before engaging with an influencer, a company needs to consider the audience of that influencer and whether the profile is a match. PewDiePie's popularity has declined after complaints that some of his videos were anti-Semitic.

Not all influencers on Twitter endorse brands, such as academics, politicians, lawyers, policymakers and so on. For this category, Twitter is the three-second message medium—straight to their followers.

Politicians tend to meet their followers on Twitter. Narendra Modi, the prime minister of India, and former US president Donald Trump are, or have been, particularly active.

Modi, who has more than 68 million followers, uses his Twitter handle effectively to communicate his messages. During the lead-up to the elections, he has used it to attack Opposition parties, but as leader, he has used it to communicate directly to the people.

Trump routinely used his Twitter handle to lash out at the media, members of the Congress, and even other governments. One jibe at North Korea read,

> North Korean Leader Kim Jung Un just stated that 'The Nuclear Button is on his desk at all times.' Will someone from his depleted and food starved regime, please inform him that I too have a Nuclear Button but it's a much bigger & more powerful one than his, and my Button works. *

While this use of social media may have seemed odd for a head of state, Trump drummed up supporters using

---

* 'Trump to Kim: My Nuclear Button Is "Bigger and More Powerful"', BBC, 3 January 2018, https://www.bbc.com/news/world-asia-42549687

this technique, because his voters saw him as a say-it-as-it-is president. His use of tweets even prompted a *New York Times* article in 2019 headlined 'How Trump Reshaped the Presidency in 11,000 Tweets'.[*]

Twitter shut down Trump's account in January 2021 after the US Capitol Hill siege, citing 'the risk of further incitement of violence'.[†]

Reddit and Community Forums

A community forum is an online town hall-like meeting place, where people with a shared interest come together to discuss, seek answers, comment and debate a common topic.

Among the better-known community forums is Reddit, which is like a vast forum with multiple interest groups that can range from technology and sports to gender and fashion. Reddit has a free version and a premium version, which is paid. It has sections such as 'AskReddit', in which users can post questions (there are rules for posting questions) and seek answers from the community.

---

[*] Michael D. Shear, Maggie Haberman, Nicholas Confessore, Karen Yourish, Larry Buchanan and Keith Collins, 'How Trump Reshaped the Presidency in Over 11,000 Tweets', *New York Times*, 2 November 2019, https://www.nytimes.com/interactive/2019/11/02/us/politics/trump-twitter-presidency.html
[†] 'Permanent Suspension of @realDonaldTrump', Blog.Twitter.com, 8 January 2021, https://blog.twitter.com/en_us/topics/company/2020/suspension

Apart from Reddit, there are forums such as Quora, which work on the idea or principle of seeking answers to questions. The answers are given by independent experts and it allows them to say what makes them the expert on the topic. For example, a former military officer could answer a question on the difference between a platoon and a battalion. An astronomer could explain why Saturn has rings. If your company has expertise in a particular area, you could register as a business account and post informed responses to questions on the forum.

Community forums can be open or by invitation only. Sometimes customers and users come together independently and create a forum to discuss topics of interest.

Technology companies typically have owned community forums, where they invite customers, academics and experts to discuss topics related to the products and services they offer. These are moderated and experts come in to solve problems or discuss topics. Some of these are by invitation only, where they call in peers to discuss topics.

A Captive Audience

One of our favourite examples of an open, owned forum is Mumsnet. Started by Justine Roberts after having a terrible holiday with her toddler twins, she launched the forum to get parenting tips from other parents. Soon it became a go-to place for parents to talk about everything from safe neighbourhoods and schools to behaviour problems. One of the threads on Mumsnet even managed to find donors for a parent needing a new heart.

Mumsnet is so popular that politicians have used web chats on the forum to get their message across during polls. Mumsnet allows sponsored content in its chat forums, which means companies can talk about their products or services, though the content is marked as sponsored.

So if you make prams, Mumsnet is one way to reach a captive audience or even engage with them by asking users to share stories that will bring eyeballs to your category. These can be done by posing a question such as, 'What else can you cram into your pram after you have settled the baby in?' That's a quick way to have user-generated content to keep the brand in circulation.

Community forums can help you manage the narrative of your brand, but because a lot of the users are genuine customers, it can also dent your reputation if the service or product falls short of customer expectations.

A community forum can allow you to tell your side of the story openly and transparently, especially in response to criticism for a product or service. It's your chance to engage directly with a customer and put a human face to your company.

Here are some questions you need to answer before you start a community forum.

1. Is my company culture open and will it respond positively to criticism?
2. Do I have the resources to commit to monitoring and responding to users in a community forum?
3. Do I need my own community forum or should I share sponsored content on an existing community platform?
4. Should I have a closed or an open community forum?

Examples

1. **Oreo Cookies**
   The maker of Oreo cookies knows its audience and message. When there is a blackout, people get nervous and want comfort food. That's Oreo. When the blackout comes in the middle of the Superbowl, that's an audience. And when no electricity means no computers or TVs, most people are looking at their phones using cellular service. That means social media.

   Oreo tweeted "Power out? No problem. You can still dunk in the dark." referring to dipping Oreo cookies in milk before eating them.

   This is an often-cited example of well-executed newsjacking, a communications/marketing term that means using a news event to shed light on something else.

2. Peanut Butter in the age of GIFs
   Sometimes a new trend is an opportunity to promote your product, especially if you have something in common with this new trend. Even better if there is an enduring social media debate about it. This was the situation for Jif peanut butter.

   As social made GIFs popular, many asked how to pronounce the moving animation GIF. That's where Jif Peanut Butter comes in. Whether you pronounce it with a hard G or a soft G, it's still a moment to make you think of peanut butter. Jif tweeted an image of two jars of its peanut butter, one with JIF on the label and one with GIF, side by side, hoping that users will think of Jif peanut butter every time they use a GIF.

Exercises

Pretend you are hired to do social media communications for a new café in your local town. Do these things:

1. List twenty global accounts you would follow, and explain why.
2. List twenty local accounts you would follow and explain why.

3. List which social media you would choose to be active on. Why?
4. Take ten pictures/video clips that you could display on two SoMe channels. Write headlines for each but change them for each channel. What are you changing and why?
5. Create a list of questions you can use as surveys or polls on Instagram and Facebook. Create call-to-action tags that will engage users.
6. Devise four ways to boost followers. Justify.

10

Podcasts and Video Stories

—Using Sight and Sound—

Overview

Audio and video content can be used in many channels. We address them separately here to explain the ways to make these types of content engaging. What you've already read about the elements of a good story, the necessity of a good headline, audience, people focus and selecting a media channel apply to audio and video as well.

Adding sound and/or moving images to your communication are important ways to boost memorability and engagement. They just work a little differently. We'll start with why and then tell you how to do it yourself.

Podcasting, corporate videos and vlogging can be done alone but often require the help of specialists. We'll tell you more about it in this chapter.

Sound and Moving Images

Both audio and video have been around for ages, but what's exciting is how they are being used today, both as standalone and in combination.

Channels such as YouTube have spawned a whole generation of videos and producers, from the highly sophisticated to the embarrassingly bad. The biggest change in the last few decades has been in how people express themselves and their opinion publicly and how that authenticity is valued by listeners and viewers.

Smartphones are now good enough for most people to shoot decent quality footage, even though phones do not offer all the functions of professional video cameras. For those looking to do quick storytelling even Reels on Instagram or videos on IGTV can be done easily on phones. While GIFs, or short looped video clips, have been around for over thirty years, they've become really popular on social media platforms because they're fun and say a lot in a small file size.

Many brands also use animation to tell stories, and some use hand-drawn images with music and video, especially when the narrative is instructive. Audio and video will continue to evolve and we have more on immersive storytelling in Chapter 16, 'Be the Story', to take you through the newer forms of video.

Podcasts

Once upon a time, you had to listen to whatever songs or talk shows were playing on the radio stations you could tune in to in your car or at home. You can still do that, of course. But radio has been snazzed up, repackaged and made available on your phone, laptop or other device with a seemingly endless choice of stories, tips, discussions, trends and good old news. You can cherry-pick what you want to listen to, when you want, stop wherever you want and pick up again where you left off. For music, there are apps such as Spotify; for books, Audible. For stories and talk-show programmes, it's podcasting, which you can publish on a variety of platforms.

Podcasting is one of the fastest-growing channels of communication. Podcasts require much less attention than reading, provide audio entertainment on any subject, and are increasingly replacing radio for commuters.

Podcasting is a lot newer than radio, which was commercially available in the 1920s, but it uses the same principles—good voice and production quality and great storytelling.

Podcasting is a crowded market. According to estimates from Podcasting Insights, there were

2 million podcasts as of April 2021, and podcasting is no longer limited to online news platforms.[*]

That's more than 48 million episodes by April 2021 All major streaming platforms from Apple to Spotify carry podcasts. And podcasts are produced in more than 100 languages.[†]

Comedy is the most popular podcast genre, followed by education and news. People listen to podcasts at home, while driving, in the gym and at work. A podcast can be fiction, an interview, news and commentary.

A lot of podcasts start off as fun experimental efforts and go on to become big shows, such as 'Call her Daddy', first jointly hosted by Alexandra Cooper and Sofia Franklyn. They called it a kind of 'uncensored, real, female locker room talk' and it got so popular that BarStool Sports bought it. The two podcasters have since parted ways but the podcast is still hosted by Cooper.

While podcasts can be produced with a small budget, the podcasts hosted by brands are professionally produced by a stack of content experts. The route you choose depends on your budget, and your ability to craft your storytelling. Podcasting is a craft, but the good news is, it's a craft that can be mastered.

---

[*] Ross Winn, '2021 Podcast Stats & Facts (New Research From Apr 2021)', Podcast Insights, 10 April 2021, https://www. podcastinsights.com/podcast-statistics/

[†] Ibid.

How Do I Sound?

All podcasts have a theme. The more passionate the podcaster is about the theme, the more authentic it will feel to the listener.

Podcasts are a great way to have genuine conversations that your brand cares about, and they can also be a way to subtly promote your product or service.

Let's say you are a maker of bed linen; you could easily have a series of conversations on how to get good sleep, what causes poor sleep and how to overcome insomnia.

Many brands have been using podcasts to gain customer attention. eBay has a regular podcast called 'eBay for business' which is full of tips, insights and conversations on how to start and grow a business on eBay.

One of the most popular podcasts produced by a brand is 'The Message' by GE. It is pure fiction and it's about a group of cryptographers trying to decode a message from outer space sent decades ago. It doesn't directly sell the brand or get people to go and buy a GE product but it reinforces the idea that GE is closely linked to technology. GE had a sequel to this popular podcast called 'LifeAfter' which showcased the marvels of technology.

Sephora, the make-up chain, did a series called #LIPSTORIES in which it got women achievers to talk about their real-life stories. The podcast was used to promote a new line of lipsticks.

A lot of celebrities and well-known personalities host podcasts promoting their personal brand. Michelle Obama has launched a podcast commissioned by Spotify. Author Brené Brown has a podcast called 'Unlocking Us', which is a series of conversations on a wide variety of topics around 'being human', centred around her own academic research and explorations on the topic.

Zendium, a Unilever-owned toothpaste brand, has a podcast called '2 Minutes of Zen'. It takes just 120 seconds to listen to. So it breaks all the rules about the typical length of a podcast but the length is a clever marketing ploy.

This is how they describe the short podcast:

> 'The 2 Minutes of Zen series gives you quick and simple wellness hacks you can do while you brush your teeth, for a healthy mind, body and mouth. Together with leading health and wellness experts, we'll guide you through everything from a strengthening squat workout to a calming mindfulness practice, all to be done while you're brushing your teeth.'

Tuning In

Still, before you pick podcasts as the medium for your storytelling, here are a few things to think about.

Why should your audience listen to you? This is really your reason to be. Why should a listener pick you from 48 million other episodes they can listen to? Are you a subject expert? Do you have a passion for the topic and can you source the best ideas and the best voices? Does your podcast have longevity? Are you able to come up with a story that is unique?

A good way to start thinking about podcasting is to listen to popular podcasts and see what makes them interesting and unique. What do listeners like about the podcast, and what do you like about it? Be pragmatic about what you can do.

Not everyone is like Joe Rogan, the superstar of the podcasting world, whose podcast 'The Joe Rogan Experience' is downloaded around 200 million times a month.[*]

Rogan does about eighteen episodes a month and is among the most popular podcasters in the world. He has aired more than 1500 podcasts since he started and Spotify reportedly paid him a cool $100 million for an exclusive contract.

---

[*] Aaron Holmes, 'Joe Rogan's Podcast Is Moving Exclusively to Spotify—and It's the Platform's Latest Addition to the Podcast Empire It's Building to Compete with Apple and Google', Business Insider, 20 May 2020, https://www.businessinsider. in/tech/news/joe-rogans-podcast-is-moving-exclusively-to-spotify-and-its-the-platforms-latest-addition-to-the-podcast-empire-its-building-to-compete-with-apple-and-google/ articleshow/75837048.cms

What also gives him longevity is that his topics are so wide-ranging. His guests include politicians, scientists, billionaires, actors, journalists, influencers and pretty much anyone who has something interesting to say or has a following. Everyone from Miley Cyrus to Elon Musk to Edward Snowden to Bernie Sanders and Tulsi Gabbard have made their way to his shows.

For those starting out, it's almost impossible to produce so many episodes, so even once a fortnight is great. Recording podcasts more frequently can get challenging because it may not be possible to keep up the quality.

Plan for at least six episodes, or a season, so you know what the pipeline is. This could help you sequence the podcast and prep your listener to your next podcast. It could also help if you have seasons, just like shows do. Plan, plan, plan or you may end up with an also-ran podcast that got a sound burial.

When do people listen to podcasts? Driving, at the gym, walking, waiting at airports, late evening. What sort of time would they spend doing these activities? Typically, between twenty-five minutes to say forty-five minutes, though Rogan has done podcasts running well beyond four hours. That isn't for everyone, so follow the golden rule: If you have lots of interesting things to say, say it. If you have few, don't waste the listener's time. Remember Zendium's success in just two minutes.

You'll need to know the format of your podcast before you start recording. Are you a lone ranger, would you prefer a roundtable, do you want to have a one-to-one? Choose the format you are most comfortable with. If you are planning a roundtable, you need to line up the people for it and make sure each has an interesting point of view. Do the research, so you can respond with follow-up questions that are relevant, and guide the discussion. You won't want to waffle on an audio recording.

What can you add to the format to make it more interesting? Can you use clips from previous interviews, can you play back recordings, or recreate sounds to put life into the podcast? Think of it as a light and sound show, but without the light. Increasingly, many podcasters also record the show for YouTube. Joe Rogan does.

The name of your podcast is a hook—use it well to bait the listener. Michael Lewis's 'Against the Rules' has a cheeky tagline: 'Don't pick sides, unless it is my side.'

It has chutzpah and works with his style of podcasting and writing. So it's useful to have a memorable title and be true to your personality.

McAfee's award-winning podcast is called 'Hackable' and is entirely appropriate for the provider of anti-virus software. Make sure your title comes up in search. Use the same SEO tips we described in Chapters 2, 'Killer Headlines', and 3, 'Story Alchemy'. You may wish to hire an SEO expert to help with your title and the description of your podcast.

In podcasting, aside from content, voice is a big tool. The host and participants should speak with confidence. Too many 'umms' and 'uhhs' will kill the flow. Don't speak so fast that listeners are straining to understand you.

A pleasant voice makes a difference, so there is no harm in training your voice or practising how to speak, or getting a trained host. There are plenty of sites that offer voice exercises.

Most reputed drama schools will have free online resources and there are plenty of warm-up exercises on YouTube, if you decide to play host for your company's storytelling podcast.

This brings us to an important question all podcasters should ask themselves: When will you script and when will you wing it?

This is the hardest part of podcasting, after you have chosen your topic. Podcasts follow the principle of invisible scripting, and need to be as conversational as possible, because that's most natural. At the same time, you must write down the elements and have a loose script in place. Again, the script is the hero. So make sure the script is about the topic, and the questions are relevant and interesting. The story should have an 'I didn't know that!' element for the listener.

Video

Video is a powerful tool in storytelling, because it's easier to believe what we see, which goes back to the old adage 'seeing is believing'.

Cisco forecasts that 82 per cent of all consumer Internet traffic will be video by 2022. Just mentioning the word 'video' in email subject lines boosts rates for opens and clicks, according to Hubspot.[*]

'Fully Charged' is a YouTube video channel for electric vehicles and renewable energy—an interesting topic for many. With more than 100 million views, it has tons of authentic stories ranging from features such as auto-pilot on Tesla, to whether electric cars can handle extreme cold, to how robust energy storage solutions are. The stuff that they don't cover in their videos such as news on the sector, they discuss in weekly podcasts, making it a seamless experience for their followers.

Video can be an important way to introduce your narrative to the audience. It can also be a deterrent if it doesn't lead to a good user experience. Let's explore what it is and how to know when to use it.

What's Your Visual Personality?

Never underestimate the skill needed to produce high quality videos, even if they are short.

DBS Bank, south-east Asia's largest, did a mini-series called 'Sparks' in which it showcased stories about

---

[*] Ben Munson, 'Video Will Account for 82% of All Internet Traffic by 2022, Cisco Says', Fierce Video, 27 November 2018, https://www.fiercevideo.com/video/video-will-account-for-82-all-internet-traffic-by-2022-cisco-says

banking and bankers, using real examples. The idea was to demonstrate how the bank went the extra mile to help clients, and how it can be trusted by customers. But it didn't let the camera roll during regular office and client meetings to capture these real stories—it converted them into reel stories by producing the series using professional actors and producers.

Video shoots can vary in cost. You can keep costs down by recording on an advanced smartphone and even edit it using online software. But just having the tools is not enough. It's good to set goals on how you want to tell a story and have a budget as a starting point to see what sort of video or visual storytelling you can afford to do. All too often an executive says: 'We need a video', when they really don't.

Ask yourself these questions to help decide if you need video to get your message across.

- Do you have the budget? Get an estimate about what it costs to make the video if it is not being done in-house.
- Do you have the time? Video production is time-consuming.
- Can you explain it in a photo or a visual?
- Does your audience watch videos?
- Does the video slow the audience down?

In television, most stories are assigned, which means they are discussed with the editor and the producer before the reporter goes out with the technical crew to shoot the footage.

Today, it's not unusual to see reporters shoot their own footage on advanced smartphones and smaller digital cameras to save costs. Many platforms call it mobile journalism, or mojo. Footage shot by a professional camera person is often called craft footage.

Social media influencers often shoot on their phones and edit the footage for Instagram, YouTube, Twitter and Facebook. They use lights and props that can be purchased online and are easy to use. YouTubers do shoots using home 'studios' that are nothing more than a visually appealing corner of their home or office, and have a green screen on which a video editor can put any wallpaper they want as the backdrop, in a process called chroma keying.

Many YouTube videos are impressive and look easy, but have lots of production hours and retakes behind them. To minimize endless shoots and editing, all video stories need a good storyboard, so you can plan your shoot efficiently.

Here are the questions you need to ask to get this process right and to be able to visualize your storyboard.

- What are you going to say and in what sequence are you going to say it?
- What visual elements do you need for your story?

- What sort of footage and voices do you need and how will you get these?
- Will you need professional actors for the story? Professional graphic artists for animation?
- Will you need to recreate a scene?
- Do you need a specific location to shoot the footage?
- Will you capture the natural sounds?
- Will you have a voice-over to go with the footage?
- Do you need music?
- Do you have an experienced video editor to put it all together?

Of course, you can commission all of this out to a professional, who will get a producer to do all these things including getting scriptwriters to write the script, but the more people and equipment you need, the higher the cost. Sometimes you may need special permission to use a drone if you want to get aerial shots. If you want to do immersive storytelling—shooting things in 360 degrees—you'll need different cameras and technicians, which raises the cost.

One more thing on writing scripts. Know your speaker. If your CEO is lively when speaking freely, give them bullet points, not a verbatim script. This way you prevent them from sounding monotonous and dull. Some people work well with scripts. Regardless, make sure you schedule in time to practise with the subject.

Short Is Sweet

Length is important in video storytelling. When was the last time you watched an entire video on Facebook or Twitter? YouTube? Maybe you watched a few minutes' worth on YouTube, where people are used to watching something.

Storytellers often forget that an entire television news story about an important event is usually only a minute long. That means that forty seconds of video is enough to craft an important message. That's right, just forty seconds.

Corporate videos should be under three minutes. Social media videos count more in seconds than minutes. 73 per cent of business videos in 2018 were less than two minutes long, and the average length dropped significantly in one year.

Your target audience is very unlikely to watch a twenty-minute video, which is so long as to be called a documentary, not a short video story. After all, a typical Hollywood movie is only 110 minutes long.

The main reason video is getting shorter is because of shorter attention spans. Millennials and the younger generation that spend more time online are used to Instagram that entertains in a few seconds. Often on Twitter, the most watched video clips are no more than a sound bite or a meme. One key characteristic of your video is finding the quickest way to tell your story.

B-Roll: Background Footage

When you watch a news story, there's often a cut to some mildly relevant video content while the newscaster or reporter is speaking. For example, when you're watching a story about the major issues to be discussed at Davos, you'll see footage of world leaders arriving. That's B-roll. It's footage that is edited in to enhance the story.

B-roll is important for any content agency working in real time with breaking news. Think about when you see TV coverage of a breaking news story. Often, the coverage shows the same video over and over again. That's because it is happening so fast, they don't have enough live video or any relevant left-over video in their file cabinet. That left-over video is called B-roll.

B-roll isn't just for news producers. It is important for social media, news websites, YouTube and influencers because it gives context and authority to your message and makes it more than just a 'talking head' telling the viewer something. Footage enhances the clarity of your message. It's used to show what you're saying has a greater impact. For example, if you are trying to launch a new kind of sustainable packaging, you would do well to have B-roll footage showing mountains of plastic packaging in landfills or oceans, to show the magnitude of the problem that your product aims to solve. Gather B-roll everywhere you go, whenever you can.

Be sure to file the footage properly with labels and shot descriptions, or you may end up wasting a lot of time finding the right footage. For example: Plastic bottles mixed with waste, date and location. Or plastic bottles being collected by ragpickers date and location, or plastic ocean waste, date and time.

Video Formats

In video, formats are important. Many things, including resolution and frame rate, determine file size. Videos can be compressed for storage and distribution.

Know what format you need before you commission a video. Here are some common file formats.

1. MP4—one of the most common formats for digital video used on Facebook, Twitter, Instagram and YouTube. It is also able to deliver high quality at a small file size.
2. MOV—designed by Apple to support QuickTime on Mac and Windows. Its high quality means it takes more space for its files.
3. WMV—designed by Microsoft and used with Windows Media Player. It has better compression to allow for small sizes. But it isn't compatible with Apple devices without the media player for Mac.
4. FMV—a format for Adobe Flash Player. It's good for online video streaming but it isn't compatible

with many mobile devices, including the iPhone. SWF was also designed by Adobe. The flash player was discontinued on Dec. 31, 2020.

5. AVI—designed by Microsoft. Its files are big because it uses less compression. But because it isn't compressed, the file will maintain its quality over time.

6. AVCHD—this is used for HD video and digital recording. It can even handle 3D video. You'll find this in digital camcorders.

7. WebM—developed by Google. This one is open-sourced and used with HTML5. It uses little computer space and power.

8. MPG, MP2, MPE—play audio and video or just audio. Their low file sizes come with low quality. This is not used for recordings that need to be edited.

9. PAL vs NTSC—these are broadcasting formats that are used regionally. NTSC is in the US and PAL is the rest of the world. SECAM is in France and Eastern Europe. These are types of colour coding systems and frame rates that matter for playback on some TVs.

Exercises

Podcasting:

1. You are hosting a podcast for an organic foods company. Craft three catchy titles for the podcast.

2. List six episodes for the first season and name the experts you could call in to interview for your podcast.
3. Write out the keywords for the podcast so that it ranks better in search engines.
4. Write an introduction to your podcast that would make it interesting for your listeners and test it with a few friends. Ask them if they would listen to a podcast based on your introduction.
5. Create a structure for the podcast and draw up a list of elements you will need—this could include other sound bites, voiceovers, music.

Video:
1. You have been commissioned to do a corporate video for a maker of gold jewellery. Make a list of the shots you need for a corporate branding exercise.
2. What locations will you cover in the shoot?
3. Who will be your voices? What will they say?
4. You do not have a budget for a voice artist; how will you overcome this problem?
5. What will be the length of the video and in what format will you shoot it?

11

Sponsoring Content

—Advertorial vs Editorial—

Overview

A story is a story, right? Wrong. Some stories are written by journalists who strive to be impartial. Some are written by columnists or opinion contributors who intentionally want to sway the audience. Still others are paid advertising dressed up to look like a news story.

A company may want to influence all of these stories. The first example is covered in Chapter 8, 'Know Your Media'. The second is called editorial or opinion, and can be written by recurring columnists or guest columnists. The third is advertising, but many today call it sponsored content or native advertising.

This chapter will look at editorial and advertorial content channels and explain how they can be useful to get your company's message out there.

So, What's the Difference?

People read stories that are engaging and tell them something new. Traditionally, information was delivered by journalists in newsrooms, but nowadays it's easy to find interesting and informative articles on news platforms that have been produced by non-news staff.

This non-editorial content can be native advertising, which looks and reads like news content, or sponsored content which may feel a bit more like marketing content. Non-editorial content can also include articles written by staff that promote a product or service, and from which the news organization earns a small commission on every purchase.

Largely, media outlets will tell readers when they earn a commission, so readers know it's not entirely without bias. Many producers of this range of content are trained writers and come from a news or corporate communications background.

Either way, they do not belong to the editorial department, but work in the marketing department or a content division that is at arm's length to news. Let's call all such content advertorial, because it's not editorial.

The truth is, it can often be hard for readers to distinguish between news and advertorials. In fact, very few readers are able to tell the difference in the few minutes they spend reading news, because they presume that if the editorial style is the same as the rest of the publication, it must be news. Now imagine your trusted newspaper raving about a product or service. Chances are you will want to consider that offering, which is why a paid post is so attractive to companies.

Still, in a world where advertising dollars are fiercely fought over, conflict of interest can creep in. Media outlets the world over have been criticized for allowing bias to creep in while reporting on businesses that give them advertisements. The main worry is the bad news on these companies is shielded or downplayed by editorial.

To avoid a conflict of interest, most ethical news platforms will mark their content as sponsored content, branded content, promoted content, paid posts or partnered posts. However, you will notice this only if you pay close attention.

Multichannel Opportunity

As a storyteller, your job includes finding the right mediums to sell your message. Since the start of 2000, with digital consumption on the rise, companies have moved from tiresome banner advertisements to paid posts.

As a result, advertorials have kept pace with all the channels of content consumption, be that social media, YouTube, online news channels, traditional media and even podcasts.

Native advertising is now part of several social media sites including LinkedIn, the networking site for professionals. Users can post sponsored content to the target audience by writing and sharing information that is useful and relevant. Sponsored content can also be shared on platforms such as Facebook and Instagram. Businesses increasingly do webcasts and live streams on topics related to their offerings and get in-house experts to write opinions and incisive pieces.

In the US alone, a 2019 survey of advertising and marketing agencies found that 87 per cent included editorial services in their portfolio. That compares with 79 per cent who offered social media and marketing. So, it's pretty clear there is huge demand for editorial content.*

The proliferation of news platforms and shrinking newspaper sales have helped fuel the rise in paid content. There are very few news platforms that do not run some form of paid or partnered content. While this makes many journalists queasy, some news editors

---

* 'Types of Content Marketing Services Offered to Clients in the United States as of April 2019, by Type of Agency', Statista, 30 March 2021, https://www.statista.com/statistics/1066125/types-content-marketing-services-offered-agencies-us/#statisticContainer

justify it saying the advertorial revenue helps retain good talent to do the stories that matter to the editorial department, and that there are strict codes of conduct governing advertorials.

Everyone ranging from India's highest-selling English-language newspaper the *Times of India* to the hallowed *New York Times* has a model for sponsored content, as do multiple television channels and other media. Not all models are the same.

In India, several news organizations have drawn flak when their journalists were accused of accepting anything from free junkets to cash for favourable coverage on companies, celebrities and political parties. That said, Indian news platforms do carry what is legitimate sponsored content, and is labelled as such.

The New York Times has a department devoted to native advertising called 'T Brand Studio'. It says, 'Inspired by the journalism and innovation of *The New York Times*, T Brand crafts stories that help brands make an impact in the world.'

T Brand uses reader insights and data to tell stories that can be videos, photo essays, reported stories, narratives and even Virtual Reality (VR) and Augmented Reality (AR).

It has done work with brands from Dove to Shell, to Google Cloud to Dropbox.

In 2014, Netflix and *The New York Times* partnered for a paid post on prisons called 'Women Inmates: Why the male model doesn't work'. It combined storytelling from a narrative, videos with real inmates, audio clips, resources and statistics. The post was placed to promote Netflix's awarded series *Orange is the New Black*. The piece, while sponsored, gave readers a real insight into the life of female prisoners in the US.[*]

In 2019, WeWork partnered with NPR's Planet Money for a nine-minute podcast called 'All WeWork and No Play' on co-working spaces.

As far back as 2009, *Vice* teamed up with Intel in a $40 million native advertising deal. Labelled 'The Creators Project', it showcased the work of young artists using technology to enhance their creativity. This was Intel's way of connecting with millennials without pushing its product in their face.

Look Before You Leap

News platforms and marketers have since discovered that as long as the storytelling is compelling and truthful, many readers may not care whether a post is paid or not.

Nevertheless, there have been embarrassments. In 2013, *The Atlantic* ran sponsored content on the Church of Scientology, which spoke about how the religious order had expanded the most since inception, under the then-leader. Several hours later, *The*

---

[*] Melanie Deziel, 'Women Inmates: Why the Male Model Doesn't Work', *New York Times*, https://www.nytimes.com/paidpost/netflix/women-inmates-separate-but-not-equal.html

Atlantic pulled the article after getting bashed online and apologized for running the piece, saying it had 'screwed up' even though the piece was clearly marked 'Sponsored Content'.

The trouble is, the sponsored piece appeared around the same time as a damning book on Scientology by Lawrence Wright called *Going Clear*. Many of *The Atlantic*'s readers felt the line between editorial and advertorial had been breached by the paid post.

If paid content is your route to storytelling, you must apply the basic rules that you would to any content.

Ask yourself who the audience is, and whether your audience reads the platform you've chosen. Most news platforms will be willing to share some basic data and insights that will help you decide whether your target audience visits that platform.

You then need to identify the format of storytelling. Should it be an infographic, a visual story, a narrative or a podcast? Does the news platform support the medium?*

Here is the catch. It could be that your target audience goes to the news outlet you have chosen, but does not necessarily consume the format you have chosen. For example, you could be an academic institution that has chosen to run paid content on

---

* Erik Lindquist, '14 Examples of Sponsored Content: Best Illustrations of the Growing Paid Media Strategy', Brand Point, 21 June 2019, https://www.brandpoint.com/blog/14-examples-of-sponsored-content-best-illustrations-of-the-growing-paid-media-strategy/

digital sites frequented by students, but are using an infographic for storytelling, only to discover most students only consume video on the platform. That's why reader insights are useful and necessary.

Whatever format you choose, for it to work as native advertising, it must be seamless with the editorial style of the news platform. That's usually the reason why many news organizations have an in-house team that writes paid content. It has to read like the rest of the news on the platform.

Most native advertising will never hard sell a product or service. That's usually the quickest way to get snubbed by the audience and lose them, perhaps like the Scientology article did. Your storytelling has to be credible and engaging.

If you want to widen your reach, you can produce the content and use targeted distribution platforms such as Outbrain, Sharethrough and Taboola. All of these pay publishers to host links on their sites, which appear alongside news labelled as 'you may also like' or 'from around the world'. Typically, companies will only pay these sites for clicks and views.

Now, let's talk of other ways in which you can establish your presence and sell your message.

Thought Leadership

Most readers think of thought leadership as opinion columns in news pages. It is that, but it's also much more.

While editorial columns are a point of view and usually reflect the position of the writer or the paper, thought leadership is a credible way of establishing expertise on a subject and creating a brand personality that is knowledgeable.

Companies use thought leadership to establish themselves as the authority in their space and often to promote the category they are serving. See Chapter 12, 'Take Me to Your Leader', for a deep dive into how to position your leader in key topics across her communication.

Thought leadership doesn't always have to be on an existing news platform. Several brands have carved out a space of their own.

SAP, the German data processor, produces SAP Insights, which has a range of interesting topics on everything digital and technology, written by their in-house experts. Their articles range from how to reduce waste in the circular economy, to machine learning, re-skilling and consumer trends. The articles are as interesting as those by *Wired* or any other technology news platform.

Here is what SAP Insights gets right—its thought leadership pitch. They say:

'We promise no sales pitches. No marketing fluff. No "insider" technical jargon. Just compelling insights about business and technology.'

Similarly, Google has Think with Google, which is a thought leadership site devoted to marketing, data and insights. And there are many others.

Grab the Expert

As a storyteller, you may not have the resources to run and maintain a full-fledged thought leadership online magazine. You may not have the funds, or even enough expert voices who can sustain a steady stream of informative articles.

Many companies face this dilemma. The option for them is to be present where they are going to get heard. Sometimes this can be by appearing in special forums and news editions on a topic relevant to the company, or by promoting thought leadership on peer platforms such as LinkedIn.

Again, you get to choose the medium and the format. It can be a short video, an essay, a podcast or even a sheet on top tips and how-to's. Your piece could be talking about future trends, just as much as it could be a deep dive into the implications of a change in policy or regulation.

For the piece to resonate, it must have irrefutable facts and an interesting point of view. It must be free of bias. And the writer must be seen as an authority on the subject. The writer's expertise will shape how the organization is perceived.

For thought leadership to work, trust and consistency are very important. Ask yourself if the audience trusts the writer to write authoritatively on a topic. That trust comes from domain knowledge. Top consultancies routinely push out thought leadership to show clients and potential clients that they have expertise worth paying for.

Many storytellers confuse thought leadership with storytelling by business leadership. Anyone who is an expert on the subject matter can carry your message. The key is expertise.

Say you are selling productivity software. An executive assistant might be the best person to write a blog about how to manage tasks more effectively using these tools, rather than your CEO. And there is a greater likelihood that they will be able to answer tricky questions from the audience because they will be the real users of these productivity tools.

In thought leadership, credibility comes from the buy-in of a sophisticated audience that closely follows the subject you are writing about.

Audience participation and responses can build or destroy thought leadership, so only those who are able to answer the simplest or the trickiest question will likely survive the audience test.

Sponsoring Research, Causes and Charities

Just as thought leadership is a great way to establish credibility, companies often pay for research to support their brand. The research could be to reinforce claims of the usefulness of their products and services, or it could be to discover better ways of doing things.

With the proliferation of alternative news, more and more companies are sponsoring authoritative research that might help them sell products and services.

Customers often do their own research before making a purchase, so it's good to make sure your product or service shows up in that research.

Sponsoring research is a common practice for everyone from the tobacco industry to pharma or even technology companies. Big pharma often pays for in-depth research into a disease or its side effects, especially when they are offering a cure for it.

Funding Bias or Smokescreen?

Typically, companies pay for research by scientists and academics in areas of mutual interest. However, sometimes companies pay for research that boosts their claims, or overturns controversial findings about their industry.

In 2017, Philip Morris International, the maker of cigarettes, launched PMI Impact, a $100 million funding initiative to support research on illegal trade and related crime. As part of the programme, it agreed to $360,000 in grants to a professor at Utrecht University to fund a study on cigarette smuggling. The university had to back out of the grant after it was heavily criticized for accepting money from the tobacco industry which critics said caused smoking-related diseases and deaths.[*]

---

[*] 'PMI Impact', Tobacco Tactics, 27 May 2021, https:// tobaccotactics.org/wiki/pmi-impact/

Not all paid research is controversial, however. Many industries and sectors sponsor research to expand sales. A maker of vacuum cleaners could sponsor research on how dust mites affect health, which could be valuable for those with dust-related allergies.

Or a maker of electric vehicles could sponsor research on why vehicles powered by fossil fuels are bad for the environment. By doing so, they might end up influencing an eco-conscious consumer into buying an electric car instead of a conventional gas-powered one.

You need to plan not just months, but sometimes years in advance, depending on the complexity of the subject you will sponsor. You will then need to verify if the organization or individual whose research you have agreed to sponsor has a credible track record. For this you may need the help of industry experts. Is the person or institution known for publishing material which is mostly accepted, even if it is controversial, or is it just controversial and widely dismissed?

Credibility is everything in research. Research backed by reputed academic organizations will carry more weight than unknown names. Besides, most credible academic institutions will have rules about accepting funding for research. Consultancies though, may be happy to provide research to those who pay top dollar.

Several of the world's large technology companies often pay for research at labs such as MIT, Stanford,

Harvard, Cambridge and others. This is increasingly the case because of the importance of technology and because, for science to thrive, it must be useful to humankind. This also has more commercial value for companies.

Getting credible researchers to spend hours to corroborate theories is both time-consuming and expensive. There are several things to think through when planning to sponsor research.

1. What's the budget and scope?
2. Does your company really need research to convince customers to buy what you are offering?
3. Do you have enough credible people or institutions you can sponsor for the research?
4. Will the agency you sponsor outsource the research? If so, do you have the details of that?
5. What's your deadline for using the research because it can be time-consuming?
6. How will you disseminate the research to the widest audience?
7. What internal rules does the research team have and how do they fit into your company's ethics and values?

When spending big bucks, measure impact. Given the scope of your research, will newspapers and social media write about it, or will it be consumed only by a limited set of people?

For example, research on the overall health benefits of green tea may have more general appeal than say research on its effects on mitigating a rare disease, which might be picked up by a science journal.

Building a Charitable Image

Companies often use their work with charities and not-for-profits to tell great stories. Supporting a cause as part of CSR has emerged as an avenue for engaging storytelling. These stories resonate with users because they can be used to show social change.

Several companies produce reports showcasing their CSR work, demonstrating that they are using their profits to help those on the margins. It makes for good reading, because it makes the brand human. Many others produce powerful videos to demonstrate impact.

The not-for-profit sector offers stories that can spark hope and enhance your brand by demonstrating the impact on the lives of those who need the most help.

These stories work when they showcase real people and the story of their transformation or change. It creates more of a connection than an expensive advertising campaign that claims you support a cause or foundation, and has become a go-to storytelling tool for almost all big and medium-sized companies.

In every corner of the world, companies get ranked and measured on their ethics, community involvement and sustainability, which means storytelling built around causes and charities is here to stay.

In India, Coca-Cola was forced to support water replenishment programmes and showcase its progress after being accused of depleting ground water near its bottling facilities, leaving the community parched. But not all CSR storytelling has to do with stamping out criticism.

For example, a cancer drug maker may support a charity that supplies wigs to patients who have lost hair from chemotherapy. The stories from that could be on how the loss of hair can emotionally scar cancer survivors, and how the charity helps them regain their confidence.

Companies who bat for their own causes can use it to tell stories through their web pages and on other formats.

Patagonia, the clothing maker, has a programme called '1% for the Planet', where they give a percentage of their sales for the preservation and restoration of the environment, mostly to grassroots environmental groups. It is now a foundation that encourages other like-minded businesses to join.

Patagonia also has a strong section called 'Activism' on its website, which carries stories on social and environmental impact and change. In 2011, it ran a Christmas campaign called 'Don't Buy this Jacket' urging people to only buy what they need and consume more consciously, literally stamping its eco-conscious identity on its messaging. Of course, this doesn't hide the subliminal marketing claim that Patagonia clothing is built to last and so, frequent buying isn't necessary.

Whether it's a cause, charity or research, there are plenty of ways to get your voice heard.

Exercises

1. List five charities you could work with if you produce golfing equipment.
2. You are a fashion brand, and there is a lot of bad press about fast fashion. What sort of research or cause could you sponsor to give you positive storytelling opportunities?
3. What are the top three things to consider while paying for research?
4. List the forums on which you can promote thought leadership for free.
5. Find three powerful examples of companies that are using storytelling to help reduce plastic waste. What makes the stories you have chosen compelling?

PART 3

Pulling It All Together

12

Take Me to Your Leader

—Positioning a Leader for the Spotlight—

Overview

Welcome to the final section of the book. This is where we really pull it all together—from story building blocks to story channels. What are the most common occasions you might use all your newfound skills and knowledge?

In this section, we identify a few of the biggest areas where you can apply amazing storytelling. We start with how to turn your leader into a story herself. How can you position her to further your message?

Chances are your leader won't have time to go through all the elements covered in this book. So we've presented it in a step-by-step approach that is shareable and sets a roadmap for you to build a presentation that will engage executives when building their brands.

The following chapters will go on to explore applying your skills to crisis management, public speaking, event organizing and creating company reports, such as the annual report.

Who's There? The Person or the Perception?

Who do you think of first when you hear these names and companies? Berkshire Hathaway or Warren Buffett? Kylie Cosmetics or Kylie Jenner? You are probably more familiar with the leaders than the companies. These people are more than people—they are brands. They have a leadership profile so strong they could be called iconic.

They are all around us. Their stories are so strong, it's hard to separate them from their companies. Everyone's heard how Steve Jobs built his first computer in a garage. What's more, his drive for innovation is well known. His brand, his profile was true to his personality and the products he was selling. Can your CEO fill that space at your company?

In order for your CEO to become an icon, she must become a personality or brand that supports and promotes the vision of the company. She needs to know how to shine a light on her profile, on those qualities and expertise that align with the company's mission and brand.

Some companies do nothing to build their leaders' brands. That's a lost opportunity, especially if a crisis hits and the CEO is an unknown entity. (Read more about crisis management in Chapter 13, 'Always Be Prepared for a Crisis'.) That's a hard situation in which to manage and build a leader's brand.

It's better to be proactive by creating a persona for a leader that is true to who they are and true to the company. Building leaders into smart, trusted human beings will help the company weather unexpected turbulence and rise faster when the wind is at your back.

After all, remember that hearing information from someone you trust is one of the strongest methods of persuasion. Who better to recommend the product of a company than the leaders who know it so well?

How do you build a leader's brand? Which leaders do you choose to build up? Do they need some innate self-promotional bent or can this be developed with the help of a team?

As we've hinted, the leader with a brand doesn't necessarily need to be the CEO. Here are eight steps to help select and amplify personalities to help the cause of the organization. We'll walk through each of them in detail.

Step 1	Assess current perceptions
Step 2	Consider desired perceptions
Step 3	Create a motto and mission
Step 4	Select channels
Step 5	Consider audience
Step 6	Collaborate with your leadership team
Step 7	Select topics
Step 8	Review and recalibrate

Step 1: Assess How People Perceive Your Leader(s) Today

Before you start deciding who you want your leader to be, it's good to take stock of who people think they are now. To do that, establish a focus group.

Focus groups are used by market researchers and political campaign managers to test new ideas and products. They are usually small groups of diverse people. They meet to watch, listen or physically test something. After the interaction, they engage in a guided discussion as a way to predict reactions in a wider audience or broader population.

To assess perceptions of a leader, build a focus group made up of internal people to start with, especially with smaller unknown companies. Include employees who have not met or spent a lot of time with your leader so they can provide a more neutral perspective. Bring in a moderator who can steer the conversation to get the leader to talk about themselves, their work, the company's work and more. It's important that the moderator has experience in interviewing, either as a journalist or as a representative from Human Resources who excels in interview-based recruitment.

The moderator can interview the group together and individually. It may be part discussion and part questionnaire. Ask questions like the following and take detailed notes.

1. What are the leader's main traits? How does that show through?
2. What are her strengths?
3. What are her weaknesses?
4. Did you connect with the leader? Why/why not?
5. What did you think was lacking in the leader?
6. What is the leader passionate about?

Now that you've collected impressions of the leader from an internal audience, if your leader is well known, you can measure public perceptions with a focus group or conduct a survey with an audience that has interacted with your leader in the past.

The goal is the same—to see how people perceive your leader. With this research, which can be conducted by an external agency, you will know where you're starting from in developing the leader's brand.

This step can be repeated later in the process after you have been building her brand through communications for a period of time, both with internal and external groups. That way, you continuously measure the impact of your efforts and see what needs adjusting.

Step 2: Consider How You Want Your Leader to Be Perceived

Now you know what you're starting with. You may have perceptions you want to change or you may be starting with a blank slate. The next task is to decide how you want her to be understood. It's important to ground everyone's aspirations. The desired perception should resemble the real person. Select personality traits that the person already has. If they need to fake it, they won't succeed. For example, a leader who secretly smokes cigarettes shouldn't try to be a promoter of air filters, clean air or healthy living. Eventually, someone will get a picture of them smoking, and that would break the trust the public has in that leader.

Not everyone needs to be a cheerleader. If your leader is quiet and contemplative, then play them up as a good listener rather than an outspoken megaphone.

Then talk with the leader. Have her reflect on the following questions and then discuss them as a way to tease out the dominant traits you want to promote.

1. What are your core values and how are they based on individual experiences in your past?
2. How would you describe yourself?
3. How comfortable are you communicating?
4. Where do your values dovetail with your purpose at work and the purpose of the company?
5. How can your values make a difference, in your work, in the world, or in your family?
6. What do you enjoy doing in your free time?

A great way to come up with personality descriptors is with a personality test. There are many out there, including:

- DiSC Assessments
- Myers-Briggs
- Jung Testing
- Thomas-Killman
- 16personalities.com
- 123test.com

Whatever the personality profile that emerges, adhere to the following guidelines.

Be Authentic: Think about how Oprah Winfrey's personality and narrative is grounded in her life story.

Own Your Space: Professor Vijay Govindarajan's passion for innovation in developing countries makes him a go-to leader in this space.

Don't Overthink It: Keep it simple. That's how Greta Thunberg has won over the world; by keeping the messages about a complex matter simple.

Find Your Niche: Know who is in your space and carve out your own twist that you own uniquely.

Provide Value: If you are memorable and useful, people will follow you.

Step 3: Create a Personal Mission and Motto

Now it's time to synthesize your materials. Can you pull the things you've learnt about the leader into a motto? What drives her? Can a mission statement be created for her? What does she want to achieve?

In the beginning of the book, you spent time assessing the company's mission. The process for your leader is similar but needs to be fine-tuned in two ways. First, it needs to align and support the company's mission without duplicating it. Second, it needs to be human and fit the personality of your leader.

Developing these leader positioning statements will take time. Having a motto and a mission that fits your leader, which is secured and embraced by the leader, will give the focus needed as you gear up for building a successful presence on multiple media channels.

Creating a motto and the mission may sound easy, but it isn't. It requires a lot of thought and the ability to boil down complex tasks to a simple and universal idea. General Motors CEO Mary Barra says, 'Everyone does a better job when they are able to balance.' She lives by that, having worked towards balance in people and between people. She is removing the gender pay gap at GM, making it one of the leading companies in gender equality.[*]

A motto reflects values and beliefs. It doesn't have to be the same as the company's motto and mission, but it should complement it.

Walmart CEO Sam Walton's motto is about vision being stronger than capital. 'Capital isn't scarce. Vision is.' And that fits with the company slogan: 'Save money—live better.' Samuel J. Palmisano, CEO of IBM, says, 'Smarter is always the answer.' And IBM's tagline aligns beautifully. It is simply 'Think.'

A mission is about what you want to do or build based on the fundamentals of your motto. It is the vision of the company or leader. IKEA's mission is 'to create better everyday life for many people'. IKEA then has a series of core values from 'daring to be different'

---

[*] 'GM Named One of the Top Companies Globally for Gender Equality', 3BL Media, 1 October 2019, https://www.3blmedia. com/News/GM-Named-One-Top-Companies-Globally-Gender-Equality

to 'accept and delegate responsibility'. IKEA leaders can align themselves with just one or two core values and build a personality and presence around that.

These are big corporate statements. The CEO should feed into the company's positioning, which is based on its mission, but be more human. A leader may say her motto is about being fit and arriving early, but her mission is about leading a balanced life and applying ethical principles. That's a leader who fits well with a sports-related or health-related company.

Oprah Winfrey's personal mission is about being a teacher and inspiring students to be more than they thought they could be. Richard Branson's mission is to have fun and learn from mistakes. It's clear the mission statements of these leaders fuel their presence and positioning. So, it's okay if this part of the process takes time. It needs to be good.

With your motto and mission thought through, it's time to build the story of the leader, a story that will appeal to audiences inside and outside the company. Start creating quotable quotes, words of wisdom and statements to live by from the leader. Collect anecdotes from the leader's childhood, early career or current situation to make the story more personable and relatable.

For example, followers of Ruth Bader Ginsburg, or RBG, the US Supreme Court Justice who passed away in 2020, cherish the story of her first law position out of school. She was fighting three fronts in the 1960s. She was a woman, she was Jewish and she was a mother. She helped to spark change with her story and leadership. Eventually, discrimination laws changed. There was no tolerance for excuses to not work evenings or on weekends. She made it work and changed the landscape for women who followed her. RBG became an icon for equal rights around the world. Her mission was clear:

> People ask me sometimes, when will there be enough women on the Supreme Court? And my answer is, 'when there are nine' people are shocked. But there'd been nine men and nobody's ever raised a question about that.*

This is how the stories and anecdotes your leader tells should relate directly to messages and branding for the leader and the company. If someone asks your leader what her first job was, will her answer be as on-point and connected to her mission as RBG's?

Here are some quotes from Richard Branson, founder of Virgin. They all speak to his personality as an entrepreneur and a maverick. What came first, the quote or the brand? It doesn't matter because it was a success. And it was memorable:

---

* 'Ruth Bader Ginsburg in Pictures and Her Own Words', BBC, 19 September 2020, https://www.bbc.com/news/world-us-canada-54218139

> If somebody offers you an amazing opportunity but you are not sure you can do it, say 'yes', then learn how to do it later.
>
> If your dreams don't scare you, they are too small.

It's not entirely clear whether he actually said these verbatim, but they appear in so many lists and sources that you can be sure the world believes he said them. That's successful leadership branding.

Here are some quotes from other leaders. Note how they fit their public personalities.

'I don't really follow trends—I don't like wearing what other people are wearing. I just like to be original.'

> —Kylie Jenner, a self-made billionaire at twenty-one who built a business on her success as one of the most influential teens ever on social media.

'Fight for the things that you care about, but do it in a way that will lead others to join you.'

> —Ruth Bader Ginsburg

'If you're the smartest person in the room, you're in the wrong room.'

> —Marissa Mayer, former President and CEO of Yahoo!

'Do not be afraid to make decisions. Do not be afraid to make mistakes.'

—Carly Fiorina, former
CEO of Hewlett-Packard

'To love what you do and feel like it matters. How could anything be more fun?'

—Katherine Graham, former
CEO of *The Washington Post*

'I don't believe in taking the right decisions. I take decisions and then make them right.'

—Ratan Tata, ex-Chairman of Tata Sons

'Be passionate and bold. Always keep learning. You stop doing useful things if you don't learn.'

—Satya Nadella, CEO of Microsoft

Warren Buffett has a brand built around him, supported by his success and his actions, but amplified by his words and his way of communicating. It's not unusual to see quotes of him speaking almost in parables, but it would be quite a surprise to see him give a half-hour TED Talk, or engage in a long-winded Twitter debate. So, his channels for communicating suit his personality, which is to be pithy with his speech, not long-winded. This brings us to the next step.

Step 4: Select Channels for Messaging and Master Them

Speaking of Twitter and TED Talks, choosing channels is the next step in this process. Not every brand needs to conquer every channel. A channel is the platform on which you speak, from town halls to LinkedIn. Each will require different types of communications, such as video or text. Many are discussed in-depth in other chapters in this book.

It's important to consider both the type of communication needed and the channels when selecting what is best for you. So, if your leader is personable on camera, you may want to spend more time on YouTube and in town halls. If your leader prefers longer conversations and deeper thoughts, she may want to start writing columns for LinkedIn, or opinion pieces for newspapers, media outlets and blogs. Perhaps your leader is really clever only when it comes to pithy quotes and synthesizing things. In that case, she should consider being on Twitter or other social media.

Eventually, you will want to be on most of the channels where your audience is. However, start small and manageable with the ones that best suit the strengths of the leader in question.

Once the channels are selected, a few quality people near the leader need to be masters of the channel. The communications manager, the executive assistant and even the leader herself need to learn when to post, how to post, how to comment on other posts, and how to engage and interact on that channel. Everyone also needs to learn about what to avoid, especially the trolls.

Channels

Email
YouTube
LinkedIn
Instagram
Twitter
Facebook
Pinterest
Medium
Company Intranet
Town Halls
Brown Bag Lunches
Webinars
Trade Shows
Media Interviews
TED Talks
Speaking Events

LinkedIn is the most popular vehicle for corporate leaders to communicate. Some of the most followed people are: Bill Gates (28 million followers), Richard Branson, Ariana Huffington and Deepak Chopra. LinkedIn has switched from writing just about followers to ranking influencers by looking at reach beyond following tags. They are called 'voices'. That list includes: Justin Trudeau, Melinda Gates and Vas Narasimhan. In India, the top voices are Abhijit Bhaduri and Aditya Vivek Thota.[*]

Step 5: Consider Layers of Your Leader's Persona for Different Audiences

Generally, it is beneficial to think of all communication having one message. Only dinosaur companies still think they can tell the public one thing and the staff something completely different—as if they can stop communication between the two. Still, different channels and audiences may require some tweaking of the message.

For example, a CEO's comment in an annual report or quarterly financial report should have a slightly different tone than the message she wants to send to employees. The message to shareholders and potential investors is about the state of profitability. A leader will also want to tell employees about the financial state of the company, but might include an additional paragraph at the beginning, middle and even the end that talks directly to staff about benefits programmes, operational excellence or new training.

[*] https://omr.com/en/linkedin-ranking-omr and https://www.linkedin.com/pulse/linkedin-top-voices-2020-india-abhigyan-chand/

These changes require editing with different headlines and images to fit the things that are being stressed for the specific audience.

Step 6: Collaborate with Other Leaders in the Company and Be Transparent

Imagine a company with a dozen executive vice presidents (EVPs) reporting to a CEO. The EVPs cover regions or products, depending on the company structure. They are important. And they are all told to get out and be heard and be thought leaders. So they go and do this with their department communication managers.

The problems appear when there is no coordination. That's when their public followers see twelve different articles on LinkedIn talking about the same product with the same angle, vocabulary and talking points. Or worse, the articles are saying conflicting things. They are likely to be followed by the same people who will immediately suspect that the messaging isn't genuine. Trust is at stake.

The leaders and their teams need to understand how their profiles and personalities are different but complementary to their fellow leaders. This should be clarified through discussion and a joint strategy, which is accompanied by a content planning calendar tool that can schedule who's commenting on what and when. It's also important for them to support each other's statements in public discussion and even engage in conversation that is public for all to see, written or verbal.

A good team has a team strategy even for leadership brands. It should identify complementary traits and spread them among the team. Building a great team is about linking skill sets. Building profiles for a group of leaders is a way to show how teamwork is stronger than the individual. The exercise of designating skill sets for team profile building can, in itself, make the team stronger and more self-aware.

They can't all be strategic planners. They can't all be smart engineers. They can't all be humorous mentors. They have to spread the key personality traits among them so that each emerges slightly differently from the other.

Step 7: Select Your Topics and Drive Execution

At this point, you're ready to select a few key topics for the leader. Pick no more than three topics to start. Decide what content to produce based on the above steps. Decide what you need to create yourselves or when you can piggyback on content from others.

It's important to remember that they do not have to create original content every time they talk. Remember we talked about newsjacking in earlier chapters? Influencers on LinkedIn often make the biggest impact by finding something well-written which they're passionate about and sharing it, or commenting on it or adding to it, to get involved in the conversation.

Some people build great followings by becoming an aggregation resource on a topic. They focus on finding the best things in the defined space and sharing it, commenting on it or both. Aggregation is like Google News or Apple News. They don't write news, they just gather it, and users go to them because they trust their selection. But on social media such as LinkedIn, a leader can share something and put her comment up top on her post for all to see.

So, execution doesn't mean the leader or the leader's ghostwriter has to be churning out thousands and thousands of words in blogs and videos. It can also mean that they are visible through quick comments, sharing other content, celebrating other events or content, giving credit to others for success, amplifying a great story or highlighting an angle from the company that's related to a story that's already out there.

Building a presence involves a good mix of commenting, writing, speaking, sharing, tagging other people in comments, and highlighting the best content as an aggregator.

Step 8: Review and Recalibrate

Creating a personal brand falls somewhere between a science and an art. It involves testing theories, figuring out what works through analysis, tweaking and trying again. Don't be afraid to review, review, review. Recalibrate your strategy and try it again. When you do this, make sure from the beginning that you have determined what you're going to measure to define success. If you don't, or you do it only retroactively, you'll never really know if you achieved what you set out to secure.

Exercises

1. Try doing a focus group on a member of your team to practise before you do it for a leader. Who will you include? What questions will you ask?
2. Gather the mission and motto for your company and its five closest competitors. How are they similar? Different?
3. Look at your five competitors again. Who are their leaders? What are your perceptions of them? Are they successful in building a leader presence? How?
4. Forget Oprah Winfrey and Kylie Jenner and look at your local community instead. Who are your leaders? How would you describe them? How do you know this about them? How would you advise them to improve their presence and reach out to you and your fellow citizens?
5. What is your personal motto and mission? How does it connect to where you work, or where you want to be working in five years?

13

Always Be Prepared for a Crisis

—Keeping Cool in Hot Water—

Overview

The world seems to be facing crisis after crisis in the twenty-first century. Companies and organizations need to manage crises, and they need to know how before the crisis hits. The communications aspect of crisis management is key to keeping your brand intact and your employees and customers on board.

What does everyone want in a crisis? Information. We become obsessed, reading how many victims there were in a hurricane, poring over stats on coronavirus cases, seeking theories as to the school shooter's motive or how the salmonella got into the chicken. And so, even if your company or organization just wants the crisis to go away as soon as possible, you need to give the people what they want. Information. The facts. Now.

How do you do that, and not make it worse? Well, communicating during a crisis requires following some basic principles: be honest, forthcoming, straightforward and sensitive. Of course, these principles should guide your communications in non-crisis mode as well, but when your business faces any kind of setback, it's even more important to focus on them.

This chapter will show you how.

Basic Principles

So what does it mean, exactly, to be honest, forthcoming, straightforward and sensitive?

First, communicate even when decisions have not been made. This is a time to reach out to your community often, even if it's just to say, 'We're working on it.' Believe it or not, this reassures your community that you're on top of the crisis, even if you don't have more information at this time. This shows that you're taking your community's needs and interests into account, gathering information and making decisions as best you can. Leadership doesn't mean just communicating decisions, it means reassuring your community that this is a difficult time for all, even you. That's what it means to be *honest*.

Provide as much information to your audiences, as quickly as possible. In a crisis, your community wants to know where you as leadership and the organization stand. That community doesn't just include your employees—it includes your suppliers, your customers and the general public. They are just as overwhelmed by the situation and by the barrage of news and information as you are, and they need information from their own employer, supplier or customer quickly and often. This is what it means to be *forthcoming*.

Communicate clearly and concisely as well as honestly and often. For example, you want to express your gratitude to and empathy with your customers and employees, but there's no need to heap on the emotion by overly cheerleading, congratulating or appreciating. There's also no need to go into too much detail when we're overwhelmed with news. Explain your decisions, offers, promotions, emergency measures or appreciation as simply as possible. That's what it means to be *straightforward*.

Ensure your communications are tailored to your audiences, as you would in non-crisis mode. Speak in a way that assures your audience you understand what they are going through in this challenging time. It's possible that your customers' priorities are elsewhere. It's also possible that your product or service is just what they need. It's possible your employees are overworked, overwhelmed and underproductive. Be understanding and communicate that. That's what it means to be *sensitive*.

All of these principles speak to the importance of communicating broadly and quickly. Even if the crisis is not of your own making, such as the coronavirus pandemic or the Indian Ocean tsunami, don't be a bystander in a crisis. You want to be the No. 1 source of accurate and reliable information for all your audiences, from employees to customers to investors. Even if you're relying on authorities for crisis updates, you are responsible for information related to your company's brand and response and you mustn't go silent.

How *Not* to Communicate in a Crisis

There are some spectacular failures in crisis communications history. After fitnesswear-maker Lululemon was criticized on talk shows in 2013 for selling yoga pants that many found overpriced and transparent, founder Chip Wilson defended the product by saying, 'Some women's bodies just actually don't work for it,' prompting critics to call him out for fat-shaming his own customers. Wilson eventually resigned as chairman. Similarly, just a month after the 2010 explosion and oil spill that killed eleven workers and unleashed 3.1 million barrels of oil into the Gulf of Mexico, British Petroleum CEO Tony Hayward said, 'I want my life back.'

Let's analyse these failures. Lululemon failed to be sensitive to all its customers and potential customers, and offended people across the board. BP's CEO may have been honest, having struggled to manage the crisis 24/7, but that very honesty was selfish, seemingly dismissive of the suffering and environmental damage the accident had caused. He also failed the sensitivity test.

During the coronavirus crisis, the UK government launched the 'Stay Home' slogan to encourage people to follow recommendations to avoid contact with others to stem the pace of transmission. The policy was later changed to allow some to return to work, prompting a slogan-switch to 'Stay Alert'. What does 'stay alert' mean, the public asked, on Twitter and on talk shows. At the time, government officials refused to give press interviews to clarify the recommendation. The slogan prompted an avalanche of memes mocking the 'advice'; posters in the same style as the government's but with the slogan 'Be Vague'. That was a failure on three counts: failure to be honest, straightforward or forthcoming.

Fortunately, some companies have got it right and were rewarded for their efforts.

Success Stories

Fried chicken chain KFC faced a tricky and embarrassing situation in 2018 when the majority of their 870 stores in the UK and Ireland ran out of—you guessed it—chicken. While the supply chain team worked to fix the gap, the PR and marketing team found ways to admit their mistake, keep customers informed and protect the brand's reputation. They took out ads in national newspapers with their signature buckets with the company letters rearranged to spell FCK. The text underneath said, 'WE'RE SORRY' and offered a brief explanation. The self-deprecating and honest tactic earned over 1 billion impressions around the world from just two paid adverts.

KFC also tweeted information on how they were getting supplies on track and stores back open with text such as 'There's gossip in the hen house. Here are the facts.' KFC ticked all the boxes with this response—honest, straightforward, sensitive and forthcoming. A dash of humility and humour was the perfect recipe, turning the crisis in KFC's favour.

During the coronavirus crisis, KFC nailed it once again, withdrawing its 'finger-lickin' good' slogan for the duration, a nod to the necessity of hand-washing and hygiene. KFC earned press coverage for its sensitivity.

Similarly, early in the coronavirus pandemic, Singaporean mobile phone service provider M1 switched its name to 1M in ads to emphasize the importance of 1m distance with an explanation: *Please stay safe by staying apart. We'll make sure you're always connected.* That's honest and straightforward.

From a branding perspective, it also reinforced the company's business and its contribution during the crisis.

Starbucks handled a racial bias incident in 2018 with surprising aplomb. Two black men waiting for a friend at a Starbucks were asked to leave because they hadn't ordered anything (yet). When they refused, the manager called the police and the men were held in custody for hours before being released without being charged. Starbucks CEO Howard Schultz responded quickly with an apology and action. He ordered the closure of 8000 stores to conduct racial bias training for 250,000 employees. He was humble, honest, straightforward, sensitive and forthcoming.

'I'm embarrassed, ashamed. I think what occurred was reprehensible at every single level,' he said in his initial tweet. 'It will cost millions of dollars, but I've always viewed this and things like this as not an expense, but an investment in our people and our company. And we're better than this,' he said in a later tweet about the store closures.

A Human Face

Starbucks's CEO did the right thing in taking responsibility and putting himself out there with an apology and a swift, broad step towards a solution. Putting the CEO in this role dates back to John D.

Rockefeller Jr., whose adviser Ivy Ledbetter Lee is considered the inventor of modern public relations. A former journalist, Lee encouraged Rockefeller and other clients to be transparent and forthcoming during a crisis. He urged Rockefeller to visit coal miners after a strike and massacre of twenty-one miners in 1914. Rockefeller visited, listened to the miners' grievances and drew up a set of responses including improvements to work, safety, health and living conditions and establishment of a company union.

Other leaders who are putting themselves out there include GM CEO Mary Barra, one of the first automaker leaders to switch production to ventilators during the coronavirus pandemic. She defended her decision in the face of criticism by then US president Donald Trump and later won a $489 million government contract to produce 30,000 ventilators, earning herself a spot as one of *Fortune* magazine's World's 25 Greatest Leaders 2020.

Similarly, New Zealand Prime Minister Jacinda Ardern has been praised for her management of the pandemic and the country as a whole with both empathy and decisiveness, without arrogance. She posts honest videos and texts to Instagram and goes live on Facebook regularly, garnering high engagement and high ratings for authenticity and expertise. She also earned praise after wearing a hijab and embracing men and women at a mosque following the Christchurch massacre in 2019.

'To me, leadership is not about necessarily being the loudest in the room, but instead being the bridge, or the thing that is missing in the discussion and trying to build a consensus from there,' she told Newshub that same year.

Two Ways About It

Consensus is key to good leadership, especially in a crisis, since keeping your community together is your main task. Community means all of your audiences; employees, suppliers, partners and customers. To show that you're committed to keeping that community together, you'll need to ensure two-way communication. Top-down communication isn't enough and can even backfire when your employees are the ones dealing with customer reactions, or customers want more detailed answers than leadership gives to the press.

Ensure your customer service representatives are equipped with the right information to provide customers. And be sure to fact-check your information. Early in the coronavirus pandemic, emails leaked to the *Miami New Times* revealed instructions to Norwegian Cruise Line staff to give callers false information, such as saying, 'The coronavirus can only survive in cold temperatures, so the Caribbean is a fantastic choice for your next cruise.' Two US Senators warned the Norwegian Cruise Line CEO to stop misleading customers, and the local District Attorney started an investigation.*

Separately, callers were urged to book cruises now 'to avoid paying more later', since the cancellations caused a 'surge in demand' for other cruises later in the year. The misleading information, and the rather obvious attempt to make up for lost business, probably didn't please customers concerned about their holiday plans and their investment.

After an initial communications slip-up in which the CEO called the virus situation a 'hysteria', European low-cost airline WizzAir did better, setting up a system in which you could rebook a flight at no additional cost, request a cash refund or request a refund in Wizz credits. The latter option included a bonus of 20 per cent for use on a future flight, an attractive option for many travellers and a cash-flow-saving move for the company. This option was automated for a time, meaning it applied to all customers, to help alleviate an avalanche of calls to its call centre. Customers were informed that they could request a cash refund later. Call centre charges were waived.

Ensure your employees have a way to ask questions and express concerns during a crisis, and preferably not only through your HR department. Consider

---

* Alexi C. Cardona, 'Senators Warn Norwegian Cruise Line CEO to Stop Misleading Customers', *Miami New Times*, 13 March 2020, https://www.miaminewtimes.com/news/senators-urge-norwegian-to-cancel-cruises-amid-coronavirus-11593151

establishing forums in which staff can solve issues together and also contribute to surviving, solving and bridging the crisis. Channels for expressing concerns anonymously may also be necessary depending on the nature of the crisis. These are important elements in reinforcing the sense of community.

Who Are You Talking To?

As with all communications, you need to map out your audiences and be sure you know who you're talking to. In a crisis, this can be crucial to your efforts to be sensitive.

During the coronavirus pandemic, many or most automakers shut down production. However, they didn't communicate that, and its implications, in the same way. Volkswagen unit SEAT closed a plant in Barcelona, making the move public with a press release that outlined the measures it was taking to protect employees' health and income. Importantly, the photo accompanying the press release showed workers on the plant floor. As you would have read in Chapter 4, 'Seeing Is Believing', images stick in people's minds and convey your message instantly in a memorable way.*

---

* 'SEAT Agrees on a Package of Measures to Help Contain COVID-19', https://webcache.googleusercontent.com/ search?q=cache:kh0jzU6unf8J:https://mundoseat.seat.com/ mediacenter_netstor/seat-media-center/Img/2020/03/2020-03-

By contrast, Daimler, the maker of Mercedes-Benz and Smart cars, announced a shutdown of auto production across Europe with a statement that mentioned 'protecting the workforce' but offered few details.* The statement attributed the shutdown not to the pandemic, but to a supply chain breakdown and the need to protect the 'financial strength' of the company. The accompanying photo? A picture of the grey Stuttgart skyscraper housing the company headquarters. Even if the intended audience was investors and shareholders, this could come across as insensitive to someone whose family was affected by the virus or by the shutdown.

Be Prepared

While you can't prepare for any and every crisis, you can put a strategy in place that will help your organization get the communications right. Start with a brainstorming session about what could possibly 'go wrong' and cause danger or damage to one of the following: 1) public safety, 2) financial stability, 3) corporate brand/image.

16/SEAT-agrees-on-a-package-of-measures-to-help-contain-COVID-19.pdf+&cd=1&hl=en&ct=clnk&gl=se

* 'Daimler AG Takes Further Measures in Response to the COVID-19 Pandemic', Daimler.com, 17 March 2020, https://media.daimler.com/marsMediaSite/en/instance/ko.xhtml?oid=45952246

Some of these events may be purposefully carried out by the organization, such as laying off employees, making an acquisition or selling the company, but they have the same effect as a crisis. So communications can be planned along similar lines. Some unpredictable crises may affect your organization only, such as a shooting incident, an industrial or other accident, product contamination or failure, lawsuit or suspected criminal activity. Others are outside the organization's sphere of control, such as natural disasters, pandemics, unexpected changes in regulations or the business environment.

Any of these can affect corporate image and the bottom line, and many involve threats to public safety. Crisis communications theory—the most well known of which was developed by W. Timothy Coombs—presents a way to categorize crises as 'victim', 'accident' or 'preventable'. These have an increasing level of threat to the company's reputation, and the response should be planned accordingly, Coombs says.

A 'victim' situation is when the company is wrongly accused of something, such as when Johnson & Johnson was accused of poisoning consumers. The cause was later found to be external tampering with the company's product, Tylenol pain reliever. The 1982 Tylenol incident is often cited as the premier crisis communications success.[*] When seven people died after ingesting what turned out to be cyanide-laced

---

[*] Crisis Communication Strategies, OU.edu, https://www.ou.edu/deptcomm/dodjcc/groups/02C2/Johnson%20&%20Johnson.htm

Tylenol, Johnson & Johnson reacted quickly. They did the following:

- stopped production and advertising
- withdrew all Tylenol from shelves across the US
- told consumers not to buy or use Tylenol until the company could be sure of its safety
- set up a toll-free hotline for consumers
- recorded statements for reporters from company officials
- launched a live television feed.

They didn't stop there. When all was deemed safe, and before relaunching the product, J&J introduced new tamper-proof packaging. The company won public support for their quick action and their consistent communication with a focus on public safety.

An 'accidental' crisis is something the company caused, but unintentionally, such as Samsung having to recall its Galaxy Note 7 in 2016 after a series of incidents in which the batteries caught fire. Samsung initially downplayed the danger, citing a 'battery cell issue'. The company soon took full responsibility and recalled 2.5 million phones at a cost of $5.3 billion, not to mention the cost of trying to regain the trust of consumers.* Samsung has bounced back, helped by its

---

* 'Samsung Galaxy Note 7 Recall to Cost at Least $5.3 Billion', *Los Angeles Times*, 14 October 2016, https://www.latimes.com/business/technology/la-fi-tn-samsung-recall-20161014-snap-story.html

honesty and speed in solving the issue and replacing the devices.

A 'preventable' crisis is something intentional, such as when the American Red Cross raised $500 million to help rebuild Haiti after the 2010 earthquake.* Some say the charity organization only built six homes with the funds. The organization claims it helped 4.5 million Haitians 'get back on their feet' after the quake but hasn't provided sufficient evidence, analysts and journalists say. The country's prime minister at the time of the quake, Jean-Max Bellerive, says the organization's claims are unlikely in a country of 10 million.

The 1984 toxic gas leak in Bhopal, India was a disaster in every sense for pesticide manufacturer Union Carbide, the Bhopal community and the environment, with an estimated 15,000 deaths directly and indirectly attributed to the leak, which has caused lasting contamination in the region. Communication between Union Carbide's US headquarters and UC India was poor, and local authorities were advised by legal counsel to stay quiet.† Attempts to take responsibility and implement changes were slow, ineffective and inadequately communicated, making

---

* Justin Elliott (ProPublica) and Laura Sullivan (NPR), 'How the Red Cross Raised Half a Billion Dollars for Haiti and Built Six Homes', ProPublica, 3 June 2015, https://www.propublica.org/article/how-the-red-cross-raised-half-a-billion-dollars-for-haiti-and-built-6-homes

† Source: http://prpractices.com/retired-Cases/Bhopal-A-Nightmare-for-Union-Carbide.pdf

the tragedy a textbook case of how *not* to conduct crisis communications. The company had had a domestic crisis plan for the US but was not prepared for this disaster of unimaginable proportions at its Indian subsidiary.

Six Steps to Being Ready

Here are six steps to crisis communications preparedness, regardless of the nature of the crisis:

1. Brainstorm, list and analyse the likelihood of possible crises
2. Set up a response team that will be activated to plan communications
3. Identify and train spokespeople in the principles of crisis communications
4. Map out your audiences (stakeholders)
5. Determine communications channels for each audience
6. Draft templates for responses to crises that are most likely to occur

One important complement to #3, identifying and training spokespeople, is to let all staff know who will be speaking for the company in a time of crisis. Other team members, such as those responsible for social media, will need to take directions during a crisis rather than respond on their own, to ensure the company's response is accurate, consistent and sensitive. With a crisis communications plan in place, the response will also be sufficiently rapid.

This doesn't mean that others can't get involved in the process, especially in the important task of keeping the community together. Feel free to think beyond information from leadership. There are other forms of community-building that can take place on various platforms. During the coronavirus pandemic, companies, universities and organizations used blogs, photo essays, video series and podcasts to collect and share the experience of the crisis and bring everyone into a 'we're all in this together' mindset.

Exercises

1. As in the first step above, brainstorm a list of possible crises—'victim,' 'accident' and 'preventable'—that could affect your organization. List them in order of likelihood to the best of your knowledge, from an IT system breakdown to a natural disaster to an alien invasion. Well, maybe skip the alien invasion.
2. Draft a press release, internal message and social media post reacting to the first possible crisis on your list. Think about what information that audience needs first.
3. Who in your organization would make the best spokesperson? This doesn't have to be the CEO or

the Director of Communications. You may wish to choose someone else based on the nature of the crisis, such as a regional manager for a natural disaster. What kind of experience do they have in public speaking and in the media? What kind of training might you offer them?

4. Examine your organization's response to a recent crisis, such as the coronavirus. As an employee or manager, did you feel the crisis was handled well, given the circumstances? What might the company have done differently, in order to be honest, forthcoming, straightforward and sensitive in its communications as well as its actions?

14

Public Speaking and Events

Overview

Events, whether they are your own or sponsored by others, can be an opportunity for you to get a megaphone out and put your message on the marquee. To do this well, you need to know two things. First, how to speak in public. Second, how to hold an event that people want to attend.

This chapter will walk you through both. It will show you how to do it in person or virtual as a webinar or digital event.

Public Speaking

Public speaking and sponsoring events or attending them can be an interesting way to market your brand and tell your story. Most companies don't think of public speaking as a storytelling opportunity, because great speakers are scarce and it's hard to find speakers who can connect emotionally with the audience.

Typically, marketers focus on events as a networking opportunity to showcase products and services. We'll come back to that later in this chapter.

Public speaking has been gaining traction in the last decade because of forums such as TED Talks, which showcase a range of individuals and their stories. TED Talks and its offshoots, and sometimes clones, have made it possible for anyone with a story and the confidence to narrate it, to become a public speaker.

As a storyteller, some of your public speaking opportunities may even be internal, such as when you write a speech for the leadership for a town hall meeting, or for an employee-only forum or product or service launch.

Some events are landmark events, created as an experience by brands. Apple does three to four events a year—from the Worldwide Developers Conference to product announcements in the fall. Everyone knows that a new iPhone is typically announced in fall.

A lot of preparation goes into storytelling to an audience. The advantage of public speaking is that it appeals to the earliest forms of storytelling and the most natural way to explain something—to say it orally. Nearly all of us have heard stories in our life—from bedtime stories, to stories in school and our offices, boardroom anecdotes and even our grandmother's tales.

Think of storytelling as an extension of this tradition—albeit with a powerful brand message.

Who Am I Talking to?

Just as not all bedtime stories appeal to all age groups, not all brand stories resonate with everyone. Only some do, like Aesop's fables, in which some stories are as much for adults as they are for children.

Once you have identified your message, you need to create a shortlist of the forums where you could amplify that message. The most important criteria here is your audience.

Choose your forum and understand why your audience is at that forum. For example, if you are a technology company that creates virtual designs for architects, do you want to be at a software conference or a builders' meet? There may be more takers for your product in a construction and building event.

It's important to find out as much as possible about your audience before committing to being a speaker at the event or nominating a speaker from your company.

This is no different from choosing a traditional storytelling medium such as a newspaper to talk about your product. Ultimately, it must resonate with the people listening to your story. You are there because you want their support.

The event you choose for your storytelling can be big or a smaller curated event, as long as it gives you the opportunity to market your product or service, or showcase the values of your organization.

If you volunteer to speak, or send a speaker to the event, there are a few things to think about.

1. Is the person a confident natural speaker?
2. Can the person weave in interesting anecdotes to get the audience's attention and connect emotionally with the audience?
3. Is the speaker a subject expert?
4. Can the speaker handle questions from the audience with ease and authority?
5. Does the speaker present the best version of your organization?
6. Is the audience multilingual and is your speaker multilingual with an ability to take questions in multiple languages? This is especially true in countries where English is not the native language.

The answer should be a 'yes' to all the above before you put your candidate on the stage.

How Do I Say It Better?

Once you have chosen the candidate, find the right story. And the right beginning. An anecdote is a memorable way to begin and get the audience to warm up to you. The reason is that people recall anecdotes far more easily than they recall facts and numbers delivered in a presentation.

An anecdote becomes a conversation between the audience and the speaker, and if it's an interactive anecdote where the audience has to pitch in with a response, that's even better.

The anecdote could be an actual life event that shaped the speaker and applies to the topic he is about to speak on or it could be a popular parable to support an idea. The key thing is the stickiness of the story, but make sure it doesn't get in the way of facts. Once you get past the anecdote, dive into the points you want to make.

The late Tony Hsieh, venture capitalist and former CEO of shoe retailer Zappos, was a great storyteller. He had a story for everything, including how he came to be a part of Zappos and why he hired his CFO. He delivered the funniest anecdotes with a straight face. He explained his customer profile using stories, his company culture using stories and his customer service using stories. As with all storytelling, personal experiences work when they are memorable. Making people a part of the speech makes it credible. For more on why this works, see Chapter 7, 'It's All About the People', about how to write about people.

Celebrity chef Vikas Khanna, holder of Michelin awards, answers pretty much every interview question with an anecdote. His most memorable ones include how he was jeered for his club foot and ended up spending a lot of time in his grandmother's kitchen, giving him a love for cooking. This has far more emotional appeal than which school he went to, to train as a chef.

There are other ways to engage the audience and make them a part of your story. Former PepsiCo Chairperson and CEO Indra Nooyi is candid about her real-life experiences as a mother, spouse and female leader and talks about work-life balance using her personal experiences, making her and her stories authentic and believable.

Some leaders often start their speeches by throwing a question at the audience, seeking a response. Sheryl Sandberg is great at this. This makes the audience a part of their story.

A good rule with public speaking is to make the speech as conversational as possible. That said, stage fright can seize even the most seasoned speaker, so it's always useful to make a note of the things a speaker wants to say and keep it handy.

There is no shame in preparing your speech and putting it on an autocue to read off, but reading effortlessly off the autocue, like former US President Barack Obama, is a skill that comes with practice. Autocue is especially important for speeches that are crucial and have a public message so that nothing is left to chance or misinterpretation.

For less confident public speakers, being on a panel at an event is a comfortable way to present their side of the story. Brands often get places on panels by offering to sponsor the panel or some part of an event. Some moderators even offer to ask questions that can lead into your company story.

The Ten-Point Slide Presentation

Sometimes, your speaker might need a crutch—a presentation. Or you could be at an event where they say it is mandatory to use a deck to explain ideas to your audience.

One of the early fans of the ten-point presentation is the billionaire Guy Kawasaki, the Silicon Valley-based entrepreneur and evangelist. He says he has a 10/20/30 rule. It's something you must consider if the only way out for you to tell your company's story is through a presentation deck.

The Kawasaki rule is mostly for those trying to raise funds for their company. It's a classic pitch deck. Still, there is no reason why you shouldn't apply the rule, which says talk of only ten important points or concepts, talk for twenty minutes and use a font size of thirty so no one is squinting to see what you are saying.*

Several top business leaders have gone a step further, by writing very little in a pitch deck and using images

---

* 'The Only 10 Slides You Need in Your Pitch', GuyKawasaki. com, https://guykawasaki.com/the-only-10-slides-you-need-in-your-pitch/

to tell their story. It works. Google's presentation deck at a 2017 developers' conference grabbed eyeballs and got a lot of social media mentions.

In it, Sundar Pichai, the Google CEO, used mostly pictures without the traditional bullet points. 'Since stories are best told with pictures, bullet points and text-heavy slides are increasingly avoided at Google,' Pichai said at the conference. You can see the presentation on YouTube.[*]

So, if you have to make a company presentation at an event or conference, make it interesting. Find the best images you can to weave your story.

You could start with a short video or anecdote and avoid cluttering the presentation with bullet points crammed into each slide.

Tell your story using data if you have to, but don't make data the story. Remember, people recall data when it's told as a story.

For example, if you were a seller of large cargo aircraft, you could tell the audience that the plane can carry ten tons of weight or two adult male elephants. Your audience will still know the load-bearing capacity of the aircraft, but by linking it to the weight of an elephant, you would make it more memorable and relatable.

---

[*] 'Google I/O Keynote (Google I/O '17)', YouTube, 17 May 2017, https://www.youtube.com/watch?v=Y2VF8tmLFHw

Events

This brings us to events, which were very popular in the last decade. Companies pick events to tell their stories because they can get a captive audience, which can attract decision-makers, trendsetters and influencers. Used cleverly, it can be a booster shot to your storytelling.

In the new normal, where people have to maintain greater social distancing, it is highly likely that events will end up being smaller and more localized, remain completely virtual, or a hybrid of virtual and in-person. The audience may be less diverse than before as some attendees may not want to travel hundreds of miles sitting in a plane.

Besides, many organizations have been hosting events online and that may soon become a cheaper alternative to an event that needs in-person attendance.

Digital events could be good news for marketers, because events become cheaper once you strip out venue, food and entertainment costs that go with hosting a conventional event. Marketers though have to find more engaging ways to end webinar fatigue and drive their message home, though smart introductory videos or immersive content.

Still, as a marketer, you need to answer why events are the best way to carry your message. The selling point of an event has to be the direct interaction you can have with people.

As a simple example, say you are interested in robotics and attend a technology event. The experience of seeing a Boston Dynamics Robot jump up on stage and grab a can of Coke is very real compared to watching the same thing in a video clip. Seen at an event, the robot becomes something you can nearly touch and feel.

If you are a service provider, events can be a way for one-on-one interaction with potential consumers whose undivided attention you will have. Either way, it is the personal interaction and the networking opportunities that make events attractive for story-selling.

Build a Theme

Like in any other medium, the event, especially if you are hosting it, must have a theme that helps you sell your brand values, product or service. It could also support a cause that resonates with your company values.

Once you have identified the theme, you need to look at the structure of the event. Will it be speaker-led sessions, will there be any experiential elements, will there be networking sessions, special speakers, round tables, product demonstrations, entertainment?

Put it all down and allocate time for each activity with reasonable breaks in between for networking. A great way to do this is with sticky notes or index cards.

This allows you to paste it up on a wall or lay it out on a floor and easily plan and change the flow, moving sub-themes around, until you get it just right.

Events need a lot of planning, sometimes a year or more in advance, depending on the size of the event, because you have to get everybody's calendars to match. If you have a celebrity or high-profile speaker, this may be even two years in advance. These celebrity speakers might be the big draw for an audience willing to pay big bucks to hear them speak.

You also need to decide on whether you will pay your speakers, as this will considerably narrow your choice. Many speakers will only appear for a fee. A celebrity speaker may charge hundreds of thousands of dollars for just an hour of their time.

Keep the Audience Connected

Social media is an inexpensive way to amplify your message during events, so draw up a list of social media activities you can do during the event, invite influencers, create catchy hashtags. To promote the event, you can create countdowns and contests leading up to the event. You can also reward your audience for tweets and retweets, or shares and likes on LinkedIn or Instagram.

Follow up with your audience once the event is over, so you convert the interaction into a more meaningful relationship. Ultimately, this could lead to a sale of your product or service. Or it could just be references, word of mouth and more mentions.

Webinars and Webcasts

In the post-coronavirus world, you may host webinars or do webcasts more often than you think. There is a difference between the two, as a webcast is usually what you or one or two speakers stream to your audience.

According to On24.com, webinars have seen a threefold to fourfold jump depending on the day of the week, on a year-on-year basis after the pandemic.[*]

A webinar is more participatory and the audience is also uplinked to the livestream. It is a more collaborative approach that requires higher Internet bandwidth.

The golden rules that you would follow for an event remain the same. Ask yourself why the audience would be interested in your webinar or livestream. You will have a lot of competition, and the audience would already have screen fatigue from work-from-home arrangements.

Remember, because webinars are less expensive to host than in-person events, they will be in far greater numbers. Think of it as the difference between getting written about in a magazine vs having your Instagram

---

[*] Michael Mayday, 'How COVID-19 Changed Webinars: A Comparison of March 2020 to 2019 Benchmarks', ON24.com, 21 April 2020, https://www.on24.com/blog/how-covid-19-is-changing-webinars/

page. There are far more Insta profiles out there than profiles of people by professional journalists. In much the same way, webinars will outnumber events.

Choose a topic that resonates with the audience. It could be a debate about a hot topic, a new idea or even something that teaches the audience a new skill. If it's a livestream, the social media platform you choose will depend on where the bulk of your audience is. Facebook and Instagram are popular and owned by the same company, though the audience on both platforms can be very different.

You would still need to structure the webinar and decide the number of speakers, the type of content and how you will keep the conversation going. Set a time limit for how long the webinar will last.

Technology Matters

Technology can save or destroy your webinar, so make sure you have the necessary bandwidth to host the webinar. Test your microphones and cameras and also make sure that you have the capacity to take on all the participants in the webinar.

Free services, while a good way to get you going, may limit the time of each session you host, and sometimes that may not be enough. A paid professional service may be more reliable for a longer webinar with more participants. Several companies ranging from Zoom to Microsoft Teams offer webcast facilities.

Lighting is a key component of how to look professional in a webinar or webcast and there are tons of YouTube videos on how to look good if you are beaming from a laptop. You could use virtual backgrounds, in case your environment is cluttered.

It's possible to buy inexpensive ring lights and umbrella lights to make hosting more web-friendly. Poor lighting can ruin a professional webinar, so pay some attention to lights and other technical props such as good quality microphones. Do all of this well in advance. Just because it's a webinar or livestream doesn't mean you shouldn't go all out to put on a show.

Ultimately, the human factor is the most important. The speaker or the host of the webinar and the participants should be natural speakers. They should be comfortable in front of a camera.

Trinny Woodall, a fashion TV host turned make-up entrepreneur, hosts a livestream every day on dressing and make-up. She streams from pretty much everywhere—her living room, her bathroom and even her walk-in closet, niftily changing in and out of clothes and adding a skincare routine, making it look like she lives in front of the camera. She talks to her audience, not at them, which makes all the difference.

Exercises

1. List the tools you would need to host a webinar.

2. You need to demonstrate a new electric car that your company has developed. Will you choose to livestream the product, or take it to an auto show? Or is there a better way to reach your audience?

3. You are an HR consultant in a technology company who is talking about why your company is the best place to work. But you are on a tight budget. Which social platform is best suited for your message? Facebook, Instagram or LinkedIn?

4. Write a ten-minute speech for a leader in your company. It's a valedictory address and you want to amplify that trustworthiness is the most valuable quality for new hires. Find an anecdote to lead in.

5. Write a catchy title for a webcast on how to prevent communicable diseases.

15

Company Reports

—When You Own the Publication—

Overview

Companies tell stories in many different ways and in multiple platforms, and we have covered many in this book. One of the traditional, and useful, ways in which companies tell stories is a company report.

There can be different kinds of reports that companies produce, from annual reports to sustainability reports, advocacy reports, performance reports and activity or project reports.

Reports are produced by a raft of organizations—from not-for-profit to banking and financial services companies, healthcare providers to advocacy groups. They can be simple text with limited images and infographics or they can be rich in imagery and light on text. Some reports may use data to tell stories, and others may use design to make the report sticky. All of these elements were covered in the first section of this book.

The report is a peek into your organization's personality but it's also often driven by budget, time and other available resources. As always, remember who you are writing for—the audience, not yourselves.

Who Is My Watchdog?

Anyone who wants to tell a longer story can produce a report, and there is no hard and fast rule about the length of reports.

There will, however, be rules about the basic minimum amount of information that must be made available to readers of the report, if it is being done to meet regulatory requirements.

These requirements are called reporting standards and they can be standards set by a regulator or a recognized local body or an affiliate of an international organization such as the United Nations.

For companies listed on a stock exchange, it is often mandatory to produce an annual report that contains the audited results of the company, and the risks, opportunities and threats. It gives an overview of where the company is headed and how it is meeting its vision and mission and keeping its promise to shareholders.

Globally, listed companies follow International Financial Reporting Standards (IFRS) that have common rules for reporting so that it's easy to compare the performance of companies using the same parameters. Not all countries use this particular standard, but the vast majority do, making it easier for investors to compare and judge them. The US, for example, follows Generally Acceptable Accounting Principles or GAAP.

Then are there other voluntary reporting standards that organizations can opt for such as Global Reporting Standards (GRI), governing sustainability.

Before you start on a report, it's important to clarify if the report needs to meet any regulatory standards and whether you have all the information and resources to deliver that.

Typically, reports guided by regulation will seek information in a certain way that has to be backed by data and undertakings. Some might need it to be audited by a specific authority.

Often for such reports, you will work closely with the legal department to ensure disclosure standards are being met, without breaching data privacy laws.

Reports that do not need to follow regulatory guidelines could mean more leeway for storytellers, but having to follow regulations doesn't mean your stories become boring. There are plenty of exciting ways in which you can make your story engaging and immersive.

Who Is Reading?

The primary purpose of your report is to inform and engage that audience. Your audience may be classified according to an age-range, specific interests, expertise or geography.

Identifying your audience will help you set the tone of your report and choose the appropriate style, elements and length. It will help you gauge if you can use local terms in the book.

For example, if you are writing a report on social development in the Indian subcontinent, and your audience is based in the region, you could get away with the frequent use of the term *panchayati raj*. However, if you are writing for an international audience, you may be better off introducing the term, and calling it 'village governance', throughout.

Reports can be conversational or more businesslike, and they can be written in American English or British English or Asian English. These are three distinct styles and American spellings are different from British ones. The key is to choose your style and stick to it.

Get It, Don't Sweat It

It's no good writing a report that is dull and hard to read. Ask yourself what your reader is expecting, and whether they will be able to skim through your report effortlessly. List these things before you start writing.

If you work for a private equity firm that wants to produce a report for its shareholders, then your audience is a bunch of sophisticated investors and not the lay reader. A report for a savvy investor need not be as simplified as one for a lay reader.

A financially literate investor, for example, would know the difference between a bond market and an equity market, between a merger and a leveraged buyout, so you could get away with using those terms without explaining them. However, for a lay reader, you would have to demystify the terms and explain in greater detail how these work.

On the other hand, you could be writing a sustainability report for a lay reader and throwing terms such as net zero-water would make no sense to them. You would have to explain that the company puts back as much water into the ground as it uses through better water management and break down the ways in which it does that.

The Purdue Online Writing Lab makes a lot of important points about using the right tone in business writing, which can also be applied to report writing. [*]

---

[*] Tone in Business Writing, OWL.Purdue.edu, https://owl.purdue. edu/owl/subject_specific_writing/professional_technical_writing/ tone_in_business_writing.html#:~:text=%22Tone%20in%20 writing%2

Also see: Scott Ober, *Contemporary Business Communication*, second edition, Boston, Houghton Mifflin, 1995.

One such rule is to remove bias in your writing. The Purdue piece emphasizes the use of neutral language. Here's what it says:

> Nondiscriminatory language is language that treats all people equally. It does not use any discriminatory words, remarks, or ideas. It is very important that the business writer communicate in a way that expresses equality and respect for all individuals. Discriminatory language can come between your message and your reader. Make sure your writing is free of sexist language and free of bias based on such factors as race, ethnicity, religion, age, sexual orientation, and disability.

This means that instead of saying 'actor' and 'actress', you say 'actor' and instead of saying 'chairman', you should use 'chairperson'.

As with all good writing, keep the report in active voice and follow the other rules that we have discussed in this book, including writing good headlines and breaking down the chapters and sections with sub-headings to make the information more bite-sized.

A Story, Not the Kitchen Sink

The next step is simply to ask yourself what your story is. This is your narrative and everything you say in your report has to be consistent with this narrative. That does not mean you have to say everything.

Lose the clutter—a report is not a kitchen sink.

A rule of three is a good rule, where you use three points to support each of your key stories.

The narrative elements must be built from the brief that has been given to you. What sort of report has your organization asked you to prepare? Who will this be distributed to and what is the message you want to convey? If it's a print report, how many copies will you need and what's your budget?

Answering these questions will help you arrive at your structure. Many people often ask the question— why is the budget important to the narrative structure? The answer is quite simple. Creative work is expensive and your budget will determine what elements you can bring into your narrative to make it more engaging. We will talk about these elements later on in this chapter.

Here are the things your narrative should pay attention to.

1. Don't make up stories where there are none
2. Be authentic, use real people and verifiable facts
3. Use multiple elements to tell the story
4. Use memorable elements as much as possible

A simple narrative can be a recap of the significant events and actions of the preceding year that a typical annual report captures for readers, or it could be a performance report.

A performance report for a hospital might talk of how you maintained hygiene standards to bring down infections, how many patient recoveries you had, how you managed costs while keeping up the quality of care. The things that show how well or poorly a hospital is doing.

Choose Your Hero: Executive Summary or Letter

Most reports will contain an executive summary or a foreword or letter from a key person in the company. This works as an overview that tells the reader what the report is trying to capture. It encapsulates the purpose and the main findings of the report in one or two pages.

Some reports skip the summary and instead have a letter from a head honcho. This could be the chairperson or a manager or programme director depending on the type of report.

A letter tends to be different in that while it will broadly say what the report is about, it often brings a more personal perspective to the report and may narrate experiences, learnings or anecdotes that tie into the theme of the report. It has loads of room for humour, observations and wit.

Some such letters have cult status. For example, billionaire investor Warren Buffett's letter to shareholders of Omaha-based Berkshire Hathaway, in the 2020 annual report, was fourteen pages long but fun.

It ended on a casual note by saying, '*On May 2nd, come to Omaha. Meet your fellow capitalists. Buy some Berkshire products. Have fun. Charlie and I— along with the entire Berkshire gang—are looking forward to seeing you.*'

And yet it was peppered with investing wisdom, rationale, tables on the company's performance vis-à-vis the S&P 500, and Buffett's take on accounting standards.

Buffett's letters are so insightful and popular that Berkshire Hathaway has published a book of fifty years of his letters to shareholders.

Longer Isn't Always Better

While company reports are a longer way to tell a story, this doesn't mean you need to write 20,000 words to tell your story. Remember that most readers will not read the report cover to cover, so you have to make sure the bits they do read are engaging or useful. A report should capture only what really matters, not every single activity your organization is doing.

The best way to write a succinct story is to choose your main message and then collect the elements you will need to build your story around it. Create a structure like a storyboard before you start writing.

MY STORY ELEMENTS

MY NARRATIVE
DESCRIBE THE STORY IN LESS THAN 100 WORDS

IMAGES NEEDED
DRAW UP A LIST OF IMAGES TO SUPPORT THE STORY

DATA NEEDED
MAKE A LIST OF 10 DATA POINTS THAT WILL SUPPORT YOUR STORY

PEOPLE IN MY BOOK
LIST THE PEOPLE WHO WILL BE FEATURED IN YOUR BOOK, THEIR ROLE & HOW THEY WILL TELL THEIR STORY

MY WOW FACTOR
DO I HAVE A WOW FACTOR? WHO IS MY HERO? DESIGN, A POWERFUL FOREWORD?

Make a list of the actions and the stories that will help you convey your message.

For example, you could be a not-for-profit working in rural India to empower women. Make a list of the activities the not-for-profit has undertaken to empower women. How have you engaged the community? And what has been the impact of the work? These can then become the three pillars of your narrative.

More Than Just Words

Once you have collected all the elements that will help you tell the story, think of what form they should take. By this we mean splicing your storytelling into different categories ranging from images, infographics, data, case studies and human interest stories. You could also add animation and videos to the mix if your company report is an e-book.

The idea is to break up the company report into more engaging ways for the reader. Say you are a not-for-profit working with women. For example, photographs of women holding discussions in self-help groups is far more powerful than saying you have helped women form self-help groups. To augment that, you could use data and give numbers to show how many women have joined these groups and then have an infographic to show how much their income has gone up.

You could also throw in a question, asking the reader to guess the monthly income of the group. It would be easy for you to build up this story with a case study when one family talks about how the work of the NGO has transformed them. This could even be a short video story in an e-book.

Using this technique is possible even for company annual reports, by putting people at the heart of the storytelling—in this case the employees and the customers. You could narrate stories of how employees delivered on the brand promise by going the extra mile, or how the company puts people first by talking of real people who have benefited from a people-first policy.

Like we said in Chapter 7, 'It's All about the People', real people make stories authentic. Always use them instead of model examples. Ordinary is believable.

In the post-coronavirus age, several of these reports are produced as online reports, making them more interactive with animated infographics and even embedded videos.

Eventually, it's down to you to find imaginative ways to tell a story that goes beyond words and is a rich combination of multiple elements from images and data to interactive elements.

Interactive Gets Attention

It's easy to put together elements to engage the reader even in a stodgy annual report by making the communication interactive and inviting readers to participate.

You could use simple tricks such as presenting facts as questions, forcing the reader to pause and engage.

Say you are a maker of microchips used in smartphones. One way to show your production number may be to pose a simple question.

Example: We create the microchips that power half the mobile phones in the world. Can you guess the number?

You could and should use data to make your story authentic. In Chapter 5, 'Using Numbers', we have lots of tips and tricks to make that data visually appealing.

Remember, few people have the patience to trawl through columns of numbers without context and comparison. If it is a complex set of data, then pictorial representation is much easier to understand.

Annual reports can be printed books and e-books, and can also be a website. In 2016, Kickstarter created a website for its annual report.[*]

The site was bold, full of simple stark messages and animated graphics. Kickstarter is a people-led fundraising platform and its messaging spoke directly to people, saying 'You made 2016 a big year' and then giving a series of examples of the projects that raised money on Kickstarter.

The Power of Design

Design plays a big role in adding oomph to your report. Design doesn't have to be expensive to be impressive; it can be simple but cleverly executed.

---

[*] Source: https://www.kickstarter.com/year/2016#Welcome

Choose the design in keeping with the narrative and the overall personality of your organization. Is the design serious or playful? Is it in keeping with the company brand personality?

Design is a memorable non-verbal storytelling boost. In 2011, Austria Solar's annual report created a buzz because it was a report that could be read only when the pages were exposed to sunlight.

Eco-friendly hair-product maker O'Right's report on corporate social responsibility had covers made from recycled bamboo and plastic, with the look and feel of its product packaging.[*]

If you have a tight budget, you could do simple things like a brain teaser or other elements that will make the report more memorable.

Exercises

1. You are a distributor of seeds. What design element can you introduce to make your annual report memorable?

2. Your company has sales of $3 billion per annum and profits of $500 million per annum. List two ways to explain the size and scope of your sales and profit in an annual report so a lay reader can understand it.

---

[*] Katy French, '50 Creative Annual Report Examples to Inspire You', Column Five, https://www.columnfivemedia.com/best-examples-of-beautiful-annual-report-design/

3. You are a maker of office furniture. List two ways that you would bring people stories into your annual report.

4. As a not-for-profit that counsels war widows, create a structure for your storytelling for a book report whose purpose is to raise funding.

5. You have been commissioned by a luxury hotel chain to make a report on their unique guest experiences. Who are the people who should be in your narrative?

16

Be the Story

—It's an Experience—

Overview

As more and more storytelling goes digital, the line between storytelling and marketing blurs. Often it takes both the communications department and the marketing department to work together to come up with content that is experiential and engaging.

Experiential content can be defined broadly as that which involves some sort of immersive experience.

In its simplest form, this is user-generated content, for which you need to have a hook to get people involved. In a more sophisticated avatar, this can be a full-blown marketing campaign led by powerful storytelling.

Increasingly, content creators will be called upon to help improve storytelling in digital campaigns, to make them more immersive. This is a constantly evolving space which will get more sophisticated as the experiences become more involved, and devices and technologies evolve. In the near future, content creators will increasingly use augmented reality and virtual reality for storytelling.

In this chapter, you will learn how companies are using audiences to generate content and connect deeper with their brands, by participating in an experience.

Don't Be Shy

For now, let's start with what is in wide usage and fairly inexpensive user-generated content or UGC, as it is called. We see these as campaigns on social media every day—where users are asked to participate in a Facebook, Instagram or Twitter campaign. It could be a poll, a repost or something more creative.

Many companies run simple storytelling campaigns which involve getting the user to take a picture of themselves and posting it under a hashtag created by the company, where the user's picture captures the theme of the hashtag. For example, #MyToothyGrin, promoted by say a toothpaste brand, would encourage users to share an image of a toothy smile which will then be posted on the brand's Instagram or Facebook page.

User-generated content need not always promote the brand; it could also promote a category such as dental hygiene, in the above case. Or it could promote a toothpaste brand by asking users for toothpaste hacks for a particular brand with the hashtag #NotOnlyToBrushMyTeeth.

In the last decade, the clever use of social media and user-generated content has helped many small start-ups become as big as multi-billion-dollar enterprises that have been around for a long time.

Huda Beauty, a brand owned by make-up artist Huda Kattan, is entirely an Instagram success story, with 48 million followers. Huda depends heavily on UGC to make the brand relatable. While Huda shares make-up tips, she also promotes user-generated content on make-up and skincare and uses influencers who try on her make-up products. Her tone is very casual and friendly, creating an immediate connection with her followers, and it has helped her build a $1 billion business.

At the end of the day, the goal of any user-generated content is to get everyday ordinary users to endorse your brand or the values it represents, because people trust other users more than they trust brands. In a way, it is similar to how many users trawl through reams of user reviews for a product or service before they make a purchase, regardless of what a brand may be claiming. User-led authenticity often generates a bigger buy-in than a traditional advertisement.

My Story, through You

Some of the most successful user-generated content campaigns have included the brand at the heart of the campaign.

Apple's 'Shot On iPhone' campaign is near-iconic because it encourages iPhone users to shoot pictures and videos and the best ones are promoted by Apple. It showcases the quality of the iPhone cameras and also encourages creativity in people. Since 2015, millions of iPhone users have used the hashtag to post stunning pictures and video. It is also a timeless and clever way to capture the additional features of each enhanced camera phone series.

IKEA did the same with its IkeaAtMine Campaign where it encouraged users to post real home pictures using IKEA products, be it a lamp or sofa or any product that IKEA sells.

In 2014, Starbucks ran a White Cup Contest in the US and Canada asking users to decorate their reusable cups with art and post it on social media with the #WhiteCupContest. It created a feel-good factor for the brand, while ticking several boxes—how we doodle on napkins while at a cafe, how coffee is about pleasure and me-time and so on.

Starbucks got nearly 4000 submissions and the winner's design was copied on to a reusable cup and sold as a limited-edition cup.

The winner of #WhiteCupContest was a twenty-one-year-old art student who later set up an art business on Etsy called Zenspire Designs. Starbucks ran her story a year later on their blog, extending the life of their campaign through a simple story on transformation and empowerment for one of its customers.[*]

Another storytelling 'experience' for consumers was one from Lean Cuisine, which sells frozen food for the diet-conscious. The campaign titled #WeighThis asked women to weigh what matters the most, asking them to focus on their achievements instead of body weight.

Users were asked to tweet what really matters to them and those Twitter messages were then recreated as wall art on weighing scales set up in Central Station in New York. Social media mentions for the brand went up 428 per cent and the advertisement promoting the campaign got 6 million views.[†]

The idea was to encourage women to choose how they valued themselves and ditch the idea of a conventional body image as a measure of self-worth.

On the day the wall art was put up, some messages of what really matters to people included 'helping

[*] 'One Year Later, Starbucks White Cup Contest Winner Grateful to Inspire Others', Starbucks.com, 7 August 2015, https://stories.starbucks.com/stories/2015/starbucks-white-cup-contest-winner-grateful-to-inspire-others/

[†] Source: http://www.alexshulhafer.com/LEAN-CUISINE-WEIGHTHIS

children with autism', 'being a preschool teacher' or 'being proud of myself'. On the first day, commuters at Central Station could stop by and add messages which were then added to the installation. Eventually the weighing scales were given away to the users whose messages they bore as a reminder of their achievements.

User-generated campaigns revolve around one strong idea and can be relatively inexpensive to do. So, if you want to run a user-generated campaign to tell your story, spend a lot of time thinking of the idea and how it ties in with your product or brand.

Here are some questions to ask yourself to craft user-generated content.

1. What is the idea you want to promote?
2. How does this tie in with your brand promise or category?
3. Is it fun to do?
4. Can the user do it without much trouble?
5. Does it have a serious message?
6. Is the voice of your campaign that of your brand personality?
7. Does the campaign appeal to your target audience?
8. Is your hashtag unique? Has the hashtag been used by any other campaign?
9. Can the idea run on Facebook, Instagram and Twitter?
10. Do you need influencers to push your story?

Come, Play with Us

There are more than 4.5 billion Internet users, and brands everywhere are trying hard to talk to them. These users are on all the time and they are bombarded by messages from clickbait advertising to conversations with friends and family to work emails and social media interactions and chats.

As bandwidth grows on the Internet, so will different ways of reaching out to users, along with devices that will be smarter and pack in more for users. As a storyteller, you will have to constantly find newer and better ways of telling your story and making it more attractive to users, and keep pace with how users interact with content.

Augmented reality and virtual reality are some new forms of storytelling that will probably become popular in the future. Augmented reality places 'content' in the real world like in the game *Pokémon Go*, played using your phone or even in the thousands of filters and animation available on Snapchat and Instagram where users can customize their content to make it unique. It could be as easy as adding a different background to a picture or a bunny nose to a photo.

It is not just teenagers who are using AR. Most of us have used it daily in the mobile phone apps that let us 'try before we buy'—from furniture in our living room to what different hair colours would look like on us.

Sony Pictures ran an AR campaign for *Men in Black: International*, in which users were asked to shoot down as many aliens as possible in their environment in ten seconds, using their phone's camera. The game closed with the option to buy tickets for the film.

Tata promoted its stevia-based sugar alternative, Tata NX Zero Sugar, using gamification in which users were encouraged to find the amount of sugar in everyday things such as coffee and carbonated drinks.

Dive In

Where augmented reality ends, virtual reality begins. Virtual reality goes a step further in the participatory experience—it recreates another world for you, making it a virtual experience which feels real, at least to the mind, and requires a headset to view.

These two forms still have a long way to go, but plenty of educational institutions are setting up media labs that help people tell their stories using multiple media, highly interactive graphics, VR and 360-degree videos. So it's a matter of time before this kind of storytelling becomes popular.[*]

The main goal of such storytelling is to make it as real as possible for the user, thereby making it

---

[*] Emory Craig and Maya Georgieva, 'VR and AR: The Art of Immersive Storytelling and Journalism', Educause Review, 8 February 2018, https://er.educause.edu/blogs/2018/2/vr-and-ar-the-art-of-immersive-storytelling-and-journalism

more believable and memorable. In virtual reality experiences, the user can feel he is a part of the story and even control the experiences he wants.

It's not just museums and gaming arcades that are using VR, though. Brands are choosing AR and VR to tell their story at exhibitions by offering users experiences such as trying before buying virtually.

Qantas, the airline, uses VR to allow customers to explore destinations in Australia. The experience starts in the plane, with a virtual landing, a hotel welcome and then a tour of the destination. Those who choose the Great Barrier Reef get a snorkelling experience— all virtual, of course.

There are many ways in which VR can be used to deliver serious messages. The National Highway Traffic Safety Administration in the US has an experience called 'Last Call 360°' which amplifies the same message as 'Don't drink and drive'. In Last Call 360°, users go to a bar, drink their way through and then choose to drive home. It lets consumers see how drinking affects their ability to drive home safely because their vision blurs.[*]

VR can be a powerful way to get customers interested in a topic. Aigües de Barcelona, the company that supplies water to Barcelona, produced a VR tour

---

[*] Sean Connell, 'The Rise Of VR Storytelling (and How to Respond)', Verndale.com, 22 August 2018, https://www.verndale.com/insights/emerging-technology/2018-08-the-rise-of-vr-storytelling

of the Earth showing the effects of climate change. Visitors donned the headset, took the (virtual) hand of Violeta, who guided them to the world of 2038, 2068 and 2093, through landscapes as shocking as an ice-less Arctic, a reservoir that had become a desert, and a flooded Plaza de España not far from the museum where visitors were walking. The exhibit was a vivid reminder of the dangers of climate change, with no explicit corporate message.

Creating VR content is more complex than shooting the content with a 360-degree camera. VR is typically computer-generated using special programs that add depth to the field of vision and allow the user to go in the direction they want. It creates an experience.

Companies are increasingly using both AR and VR to sell products by experiencing them. IKEA has a VR experience which lets you be in the IKEA space you want and experience it like you would in real life. You could also go a step further and change the colours of say a kitchen door, open the kitchen shelves and place pots and pans inside it to see how much it would hold, all with a headset on.

The BBC Academy has a good module on VR which is a must-read for beginners and covers a range of issues including cost of production.[*]

---

[*] 'Virtual Reality Production: Where Do I Start?', BBC, https://www.bbc.com/academy-guides/virtual-reality-production-where-do-i-start

Before you tell your story through a VR experience, here are the things that you must consider according to the BBC Academy guide.

1. How will people see this experience? What size is that audience?
2. What platforms will this experience be made for?
3. How will you build this experience technically?
4. Is the budget realistic for what you want to produce? Is there time and money built in for prototyping and user testing?
5. If you are using a VR company, has it got a good track record in making VR experiences?
6. Once you have finished the project, how will you distribute and promote it?

This is just a starting point, because we are still in the early stages of VR at the start of this decade. Just like AR is a quick fun way to engage users, VR too may one day become as commonplace as AR. In fact, for those born in this decade, it may be the primary way they understand stories—by experiencing them.

Exercises

1. Create a user-generated Instagram campaign for a brand of breakfast cereal.
2. What's your catchy hashtag?
3. Will you use augmented reality for the storytelling?

4. If the answer to question 3 is yes, what is the AR element and how it will create more awareness and connection for your brand?
5. If the answer to question 3 is no, then create a storyboard with three different endings for a VR campaign for your brand.